Electric Kiln Ceramics *A Potter's Guide to Clays and Glazes*

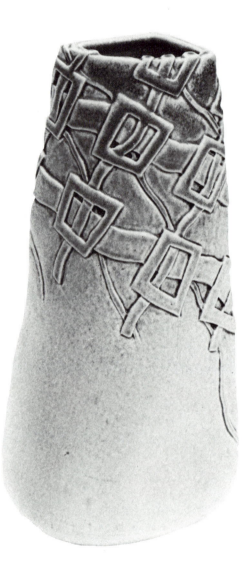

Electric Kiln Ceramics

A Potter's Guide to Clays and Glazes

Richard Zakin

CHILTON BOOK COMPANY / RADNOR, PENNSYLVANIA

Cover: Adelaide Alsop Robineau. *Reticulated Jar.* This piece was
fired in the oxidizing atmosphere of a fuel-burning muffle kiln.
The muffle kiln was developed to a state of technical perfection
in the early twentieth century. In this design, the ware and the
flame are separated by a refractory wall: the ware is heated by
radiation and conduction rather than by direct exposure to the
flame. The muffle kiln, with its oxidizing atmosphere and
indirect heat, was the direct ancestor of the modern electric kiln.
Courtesy of The Smithsonian Institution, Washington, D.C.

Title page: Richard Zakin. Porcelainous clay body. Cone 6.

1 2 3 4 5 6 7 8 9 0   0 9 8 7 6 5 4 3 2 1

Jean Delius was the first person to encourage me to write this book.
Jean was a constant source of advice and encouragement to many
in the crafts, including me.
When I ran into the inevitable problems, she quietly and
steadily came to my aid.
This book is dedicated to her memory.

Contents

Acknowledgments

I wish to acknowledge the help of the President and the Dean of Arts and Sciences of the State University of New York at Oswego who allowed me to take a leave so that I could finish this book.

I would also like to thank William Hunt, Managing Editor of *Ceramics Monthly* magazine, for his useful advice and warm encouragement, and my teachers at Alfred with a special note of gratitude to William Parry, professor of sculpture at Alfred, whose restless curiosity and inventive approach to ceramic problems have always been a great source of inspiration.

Don Gauthier, an instructor at Oswego from 1976 to 1978, deserves a special mention for his help with the section on oxidation firing in a gas kiln.

I also want to thank my photographer, Thomas Eckersley. While many of the photographs in this book were taken by him, this is only part of the story. Tom served as my photographic adviser, and his aid was invaluable.

The following formulas first appeared in an article I wrote for *Ceramics Review* magazine: August Tan Fineclay, Brutus Base I and II, Chenies Base, Coburg Base, Dolomite White Body, Drummond Base, Gardington Base, Gower Base, Karen's Glaze, Satin Mat I and II, Troy IV Base, and U.B. I White Fineclay. The formulas for Huntley Engobe and Pumice Glaze also appeared in *Ceramics Review* in slightly different form. Other formulas have appeared in *Ceramics Monthly*. I extend my deep appreciation for permission to reprint them all here.

Electric Kiln Ceramics   *A Potter's Guide to Clays and Glazes*

Introduction

This book is intended for the potter who wishes to use the oxidizing electric kiln to its fullest potential. Compared to fuel-burning kilns, the electric kiln is a recent invention, and we still are finding out how best to use it. In the past thirty years, the electric kiln has become popular because of its convenience, safety, and economy. For best results, however, the potter using the electric kiln should employ clay bodies and glazes suitable to the electric fire. Because the electric kiln is different from all other kilns, a whole new spectrum of formulas and procedures must be worked out. Older recipes and techniques that work beautifully with fuel-burning kilns tend to produce pallid, bland results in the electric fire.

Therefore, the formulas and procedures in this book have been tailored to the requirements of the electric fire. It is my hope they will help many potters obtain work of the highest quality from this remarkable kiln.

The electric kiln's oxidation fire differs significantly from the reduction fire produced by fuel-burning kilns. Reduction firing has dominated Western pottery for the last half-century, and consequently we tend to think of oxidation firing as a recent innovation, viewed in many circles as the poor cousin of the reduction fire. But, in fact, the firing of oxidation stoneware and porcelain has a long history in Europe, the Middle East, and Asia. That for 1000 years Asia has produced high-fired oxidation ware in great quantity is surprising to many potters.

The work of the Tzu Chou potters of China is a fine example of the high-fired oxidation ware typical of the Sung dynasty and later. This technique, which is perfectly suited to the character of the oxidation fire, relies for its

1

Taxile Doat (ca. 1900). Sèvres, France. *Dish with White and Green Cameo*. This piece was fired in oxidation in a fuel-burning kiln. The softness of the flowing mat glazes is contrasted with the hard-edged character of the cameolike imagery of the paté sur paté medallion. Taxile Doat wrote an influential technical treatise in the early 1900s known in English as "Grand Feu Ceramics." *Courtesy of The Cleveland Museum of Art, Purchase, Sundry Purchase Fund*

2

Rookwood (1921). Cincinnati, Ohio. Although the techniques used to glaze these pieces were secret, we can deduce some technical material from the evidence of the pots themselves. The pieces are oxidation fired. The body is white and opaque, a white fineclay. The yellow glaze was probably derived from a vanadium stain. Because of the way the glaze falls away from the edges and raised areas of the piece, it seems most likely that the glaze was a high flux, flowing mat glaze; this type of formula was very popular at the turn of the century. The hard, durable surface of the glaze suggests the presence of zinc, titanium, and perhaps nickel. Both the dense white body and the smooth durable mat glaze suggest that the piece was fired in the mid- or high-fire ranges. *Private collection*

Rookwood (1923). Cincinnati, Ohio. Here too the glaze (in this case a soft turquoise color) is textured in such a way as to suggest a flowing mat formula. Much excess glaze flow at the foot corroborates this. Unlike many flowing mat glazes, this is very smooth and durable. *Private collection*

Adelaide Alsop Robineau (1865–1929). Syracuse, New York. Cone 9. Robineau lived and worked in Syracuse from the turn of the century until 1929. Most of her work was fired in oxidation. This piece is glazed with a low alumina, flowing mat formulation. The body is porcelain. *Courtesy of the Everson Museum, Syracuse, New York*

Adelaide Alsop Robineau. Syracuse, New York. Cone 9. This is a porcelain piece with a low alumina glaze containing titanium, zinc, or a combination of the two. It has been fired so as to encourage the growth of metallic crystals on the surface of the piece. The crystals are visible on the side. *Courtesy of the Everson Museum, Syracuse, New York*

effect on the dark slips and light bodies so familiar to the oxidation worker. In this book I explain how contemporary potters can achieve the same effects in the electric kiln.

Potters who worked extensively in Japan have often described oxidation firings and glazes that we in the West associate closely with reduction firing. One fine type of pottery from Japan is an oxidation-type Oribe ware, which like Tzu Chou ware is well suited to the character of oxidation. Strong in color and graphic in character, Oribe pottery shows a daring and inventive imagery unique in Japanese ceramics.

In Europe, oxidation was the accepted method of firing for many centuries. Although some of these porcelain and stoneware oxidation styles do not have much current appeal, we can appreciate the work of late nineteenth- and twentieth-century figures such as Ernest Chaplet, August Delaherche, Jean Carries, and Taxile Doat. Their work is inventive and features rich, textured surfaces.

In the United States, Adelaide Alsop Robineau, F. H. Rhead, and Arthur Baggs all worked primarily in high-fire oxidation. Robineau's exceptional work in carved ware, with crystal and flowing glazes, was fired in a cone 9 oxidation fuel-burning kiln. After many years of neglect, her work again is attracting widespread interest and admiration. Much of this interest may be attributed to the graphic characteristics of oxidation-fired ware.

Potters in our time have become used to choosing from a broad range of handsome, reliable bodies and glazes, especially for cone 9 and 10 reduction. At present, we are in the process of developing equivalent bodies and glazes for oxidation-fired ware. This is an exciting time for potters working with the electric kiln, a time of development for them as well as for their work. I believe that oxidation firing is in the same position now as salt firing was in the early sixties: poised on the edge of a great revival, with its most rewarding secrets still to be discovered and its greatest work yet to be created.

1 *The Electric Kiln*

The term atmosphere refers to the character of the environment inside the kiln chamber during firing. Electric firing produces an atmosphere known as oxidizing. Fuel-burning kilns can produce either oxidizing or reducing kiln atmospheres. In the reducing fire, the flow of air entering the firing chamber is impeded, thereby creating an oxygen-poor atmosphere in the chamber. In the oxidizing fire, on the other hand, air is allowed easy access to the firing chamber, and the atmosphere inside the chamber is amply supplied with oxygen at all times. The difference between these two methods has a profound influence on the look of the fired object.

In the oxidizing fire, any iron compounds in the clay body take the form of red iron oxide (Fe_2O_3). These color the clay body red, brown, or tan. Titanium compounds (common and influential clay body impurities) turn clay bodies ochre or gray ochre in the oxidation fire. The oxidation fire discourages the concentration of melted specks of black iron oxide, titanium, and other impurities, which express themselves as the irregularly spotted texture characteristic of reduction-fired clay bodies. Oxidation-fired clay bodies are smooth and uniform in texture.

The oxidation fire influences glaze color as well. Iron oxide tends to produce soft earth colors, coloring the glaze tan, green-tan, brown, or brick. Titanium colors glazes yellow or gray-yellow. Copper colors glazes green or aqua blue (never the oxblood red characteristic of reduction). Cobalt colors glazes blue (often a cooler, more pleasant blue than the harsh, warm blue of cobalt fired in reduction).

Firing atmosphere influences the visual texture of the glaze as well as the clay body. In the reduction fire, the irregularly spotted texture of the body carries through the glaze, especially where the glaze is thin. Reduction-fired surfaces tend toward saturated and broken color, with strong visual texture. Oxidation-fired surfaces do not have this sort of visual texture; they are often smooth and unbroken, and in many cases less rich.

The challenge for the oxidation potter is to give clay bodies and glazes a quality of richness and individual character.

COMPARISONS OF OXIDATION AND REDUCTION

Oxidation	*Reduction*
Clay bodies	
unbroken color; light buff, tan and red tan	broken color, iron spots; gray, gray-tan, rich browns
Glaze texture	
unbroken color; glazes in oxidation are most often flat and smooth	broken color; in reduction, glazes usually "break up"; different colors are produced depending on glaze thickness
Glaze surface	
dry, mat, satin, smooth, or shiny	same
Glaze colors	
white, gray, black, orange, brown, yellow, blue, green, and iron red	white, gray, black, orange, brown, brown-red, oxblood, iron red, and blue
Overall character	
simple and unbroken glaze surfaces well adapted to complex glaze application and manipulation; in this way the potter can achieve rich and broken textures	complicated and broken glaze surfaces well adapted to simple and direct glaze applications; natural rich and broken textures are produced

The electric kiln normally can be used only for oxidation firing, whereas the fuel-burning kiln can be used for either oxidation or reduction firing. It would seem therefore that the fuel-burning kiln is preferable because it is not as limited as the electric kiln. The electric kiln, however, has great advantages for the potter who fires in oxidation:

Initial expense. Electric kilns may be purchased or built inexpensively. They are less expensive than any except the most rudimentary fuel-burning kilns.

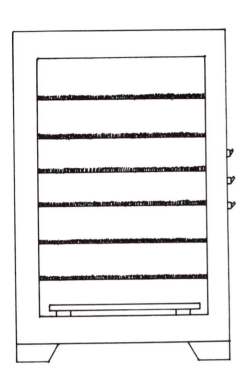

ELECTRIC KILN

Electric current + resistance = heat

In the electric kiln, heat is produced by resistance to a current through a coil.

Advantages:
1. Safety
2. Ease of firing
3. Compactness
4. Cleanliness
5. Economy

Disadvantages:
1. No reduction (in the classical sense)

COMBUSTION KILN

Fuel (wood, gas, oil, propane) + oxygen = combustion (heat)

In the fuel-burning kiln, heat is produced by a flame.

Advantages:
1. Flexibility: the kiln may be fired in oxidation or reduction

Disadvantages:
1. Time consuming to fire
2. Not as clean as an electric kiln

1-1   Electric kiln.

1-2   Combustion kiln.

Repair. Electric kilns last a long time with very little repair. Elements occasionally may need to be replaced, as perhaps will a few bricks, but a kiln that has been fired carefully will need little upkeep.

Operating expense. Electric kilns cost less to fire per useful cubic foot than do most fuel-burning kilns. At one time most fuels were relatively inexpensive, and the potter who fired in the electric kiln was at an economic disadvantage. Electric power rates have not risen as drastically as have other fuels, however, and this difference in costs no longer exists.

Safety. Although no kiln is entirely safe, the electric kiln is much safer than fuel-burning kilns. Safety equipment is incorporated easily into the construction of new electric kilns and into electric kilns already in use. Safety devices are far less intrusive in the electric kiln than in the fuel-burning kiln. Safety devices for the electric kiln are simple, positive, and fairly inexpensive.

Placement. Electric kilns may be placed safely in areas where fuel-burning kilns are a problem, such as near living quarters and in classrooms. Electric kilns do not need to be placed in a kiln shed.

Noise. Electric kilns are quiet. They do not have the drama of the gas kiln, but they are much easier to live with and to work around.

Size. Electric kilns are much more compact than most fuel-burning kilns.

Smoke. Electric kilns do not need stacks, do not issue flame or smoke, and do not call attention to themselves. This is most useful, especially in crowded urban and suburban areas. The advent of the urban potter may have a profound influence on the future course of ceramics.

Electric kilns come in many sizes and types. The two main classes are the front-loading kiln and the top-loading kiln. The top-loading kiln is relatively inexpensive and simple to build; the front loader needs massive bracing around the door and flexible connections from the electrical harness to the door elements, which make it more expensive. The top loader, however, is more difficult to load than the front-loading kiln, especially in large kilns.

Other distinctions can be made. Many electric kilns are thin-walled, with the bricks stacked on end. Other kilns are made with the bricks stacked on their sides, which gives a thicker wall and better insulation.

Today many top-loading kilns are hexagonal in shape. In this type of kiln, the brick is stacked on end. Choose one of these only if it has a good system of supplementary insulation.

Some top-loading kilns come apart; this can be a source of heat loss unless some provision is made to prevent it, frequently with Kaowool rope.

A well-made electric kiln offers a nice balance of flexibility, simplicity, and reliability. Remember that all types of kilns can be built well or poorly. Do not be fooled by a shiny exterior. Rather, look for good wiring, strong bracing, and effective insulation.

Some Notes on Glaze Firing

Out of convenience and environmental considerations, most potters do their oxidation work in the electric kiln. Because they have only narrow experience in kiln firing, and as the electric kiln seems so simple to fire, it never occurs to them to experiment with different firing procedures. With a few simple changes in firing, most oxidation potters will see a vast improvment in the quality of their glazes.

The following suggestions are useful:

Cones. Always fire with cones. They are the only really accurate indication of what is happening to the glazes inside the kiln.

Kiln sitters. Just as no potter would expect to fire a fuel-burning kiln automatically, neither should the electric kiln be fired automatically. Kiln sitters have their place, but they are misused when they replace human judgment. If you have a sitter, use it as a backup safety device. For example, if you are firing to cone 6, put a cone 8 in the sitter to prevent gross overfiring. Meanwhile, use normal cones, placing them in front of the spyhole; when they fall, you will know that firing temperature has been reached. It is easy to fire down at this point, which is not true of a kiln that has been fired automatically.

Firing down. To fire down is to leave the kiln on a low heat setting after the cone has fallen and the kiln has reached temperature. Rather than turning the kiln off entirely, the potter leaves one switch on, or leaves a few switches on low. Instead of cooling quickly, the kiln looses heat slowly. In this way the glazes have a chance to develop beautiful visual textures with microcrystalline activity on the surface. These crystals will not form if the glaze is allowed to cool rapidly.

Care of the Electric Kiln

1. Test the kiln elements regularly. A small piece of Styrofoam is a fine element tester. Turn on all switches on the kiln. Place the Styrofoam on each element in turn. If the element is working, the Styrofoam will melt slightly and indent; if this does not happen, the element is broken or disconnected.

2. Clean the kiln regularly with a vacuum cleaner.

3. Leave the kiln door ajar in the early part of the firing so that moisture and smoke may be vented without harming the elements and the kiln.

4. Replace broken or crumbling bricks.

5. Make sure that smoky materials, such as sawdust or newspapers, are not fired in the electric kiln. Avoid bodies that are "loaded" with these materials.

6. Do not attempt to reduce electric kilns by introducing burnable materials into the firing chamber unless the kiln is specifically designed for reduction.

7. Do not jostle the kiln elements. They become brittle as they age.

REPAIRING SAGGING ELEMENTS

A sagging element should never be repaired when the element is cold and brittle. Turn the element on and let it get hot. Then, with two scrap pieces of wood (no metal should be used), force the expanded, sagging elements closer together and up into their proper channel. Patience and care are required for this operation.

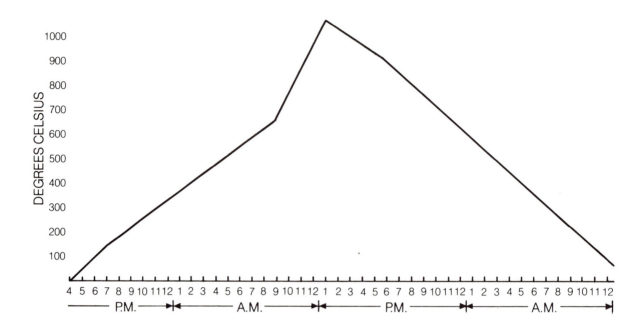

4:00 P.M.	The kiln is started. Two switches are turned on (low setting), and the kiln door is left ajar.
7:00 P.M.	The kiln door is closed.
9:00 A.M.	The kiln has been on low heat overnight. Now the kiln is above red heat at about 600°C. Two more switches are turned on (medium high setting).
9:10 A.M.	The rest of the switches are turned on (high setting).
12:30 P.M.	The kiln reaches maturity. All switches but one are turned off (very low setting). The kiln is fired down.
5:30 P.M.	The last switch is turned off.
9:00 A.M.	The next morning the kiln plugs are removed.
10:30 A.M.	The kiln door is opened and left ajar.
12:30 P.M.	The kiln is unloaded.

1-3   A typical electric bisque fire (cone 06).

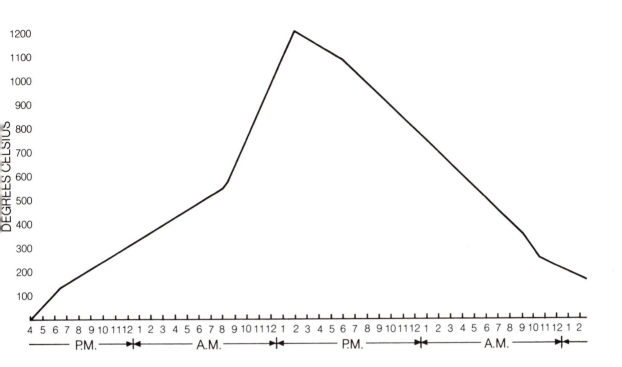

4:00 P.M.	The kiln is started. Two switches are turned on (low setting). The kiln door is left ajar.
6:30 P.M.	The kiln door is closed.
8:00 A.M.	The kiln has been on a low heat setting overnight. The next morning, the kiln is above red heat, 550°C. Two more switches are turned on (medium high setting).
8:20 A.M.	The rest of the switches are turned on (high setting).
2:00 P.M.	The kiln reaches maturity. All switches *but one* are turned off (very low setting). The kiln is fired down.
6:00 P.M.	The last switch is turned off.
9:00 A.M.	The next morning the kiln plugs are removed.
10:30 A.M.	The door is opened slightly and left ajar.
2:30 P.M.	The kiln is unloaded.

1-4   A typical electric high fire (cone 6).

REPLACING BROKEN ELEMENTS

Even with careful use, kiln elements eventually will break. At that point the element will no longer pass any current and must be replaced. Though each brand of kiln has a different arrangement, the practice is generally the same. The kiln elements, in their channel in the wall, go around the firing chamber once or twice. The ends of the elements go through the walls to a wiring harness suspended on the outside of the kiln. After the broken coil is pulled out of the channel and unhooked from the wiring harness, the new coil is placed in the channel and the ends are connected to the harness.

Building Your Own Kiln

Although there are many fine manufactured electric kilns on the market, many selling for very reasonable prices, some potters choose to build their kiln rather than buy it. Electric kilns do not present great difficulties in construction; the most difficult aspect is obtaining the proper length Kanthal kiln elements. Building a kiln is a time-consuming process, but the kiln that is built by the potter is often stronger and more efficient than a factory model. Money saved varies from one-third to one-half the price of a new kiln.

Perhaps the best reason for building your own kiln is the knowledge gained in the process. Since manufactured models are inexpensive, only acquiring this knowledge can compensate for the hours spent on kiln construction. For many potters and teachers, however, this is valuable knowledge.

A kiln kit is an excellent compromise. It supplies the Kanthal elements, the hardware, and all specifications and measurements; the labor and the locally available soft brick and insulation are provided by the potter.

The best current book on all aspects of electric kiln construction is Robert Fournier, *Electric Kiln Construction for Potters* (New York: Van Nostrand Reinhold, 1977).

Oxidation Firing in the Fuel-Burning Kiln

Although oxidation firing is usually associated with the electric kiln, it can be accomplished very well in a fuel-burning kiln. There are, in fact, a number of good reasons for firing in oxidation, even in a kiln that has a selection of firing atmospheres.

Oxidation is an efficient, economical way to fire. Many kilns fire better in oxidation than they do in reduction. One brand of prebuilt gas kiln, which is famous in the profession for firing problems, fires quite well in oxidation. And oxidation firing produces graphic quality and brilliantly saturated color effects.

AN OXIDATION FIRING IN A GAS KILN

In October 1977, we fired an Alpine Updraft Ten-Cubic-Foot natural gas kiln to cone 6 in an oxidation atmosphere. We found that this kiln fired very well

14

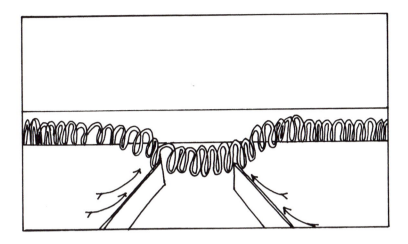

1-5 Push a sagging element into place with two pieces of wood.

1-6 Cross section showing element wiring.

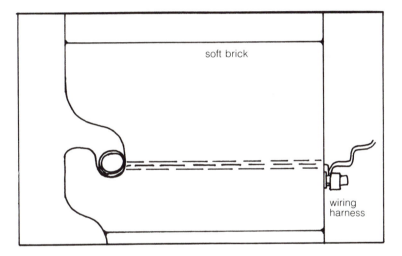

soft brick

wiring harness

in oxidation; the fire was even, and, if anything, went too quickly. Although every gas kiln is different, it may be useful here to include firing information for a natural gas oxidation fire. Any aspirator burner (blower driven) updraft kiln should follow this pattern fairly closely. Inspirator (nonblower driven) burner or downdraft kilns may need a different firing pattern.

Time	Flame	Blowers	Damper
8:00	start pilots only	off	½ open
8:30	burners on ½ inch gas pressure	on ⅓ full speed	½ open
9:00	burners on 1 inch gas pressure	on ⅓ full speed	½ open
9:30	burners on 1.5 inches gas pressure	on ⅓ full speed	½ open
10:00	burners on 2 inches of gas pressure	on ⅔ full speed	½ open
10:30	burners on 2.5 inches of gas pressure	on ⅔ full speed	½ open
11:00	red heat: burners on 3.5 inches of gas pressure	on top speed	⅓ open

The flame should be short and a brilliant light blue-green. There should be no back pressure (indicated by a flame pushing out of the damper or other openings).

If the kiln has been fired in a reduction atmosphere and you wish to fire in oxidation, one or two bisque kilns should be fired to clear the bricks and kiln furniture of any lingering effects of reduction. The kiln is loaded normally with good heat circulation. If you expect much oxidation firing, switch to cordierite shelves, which last longer in oxidation than do silicon carbide shelves. Because this is a very efficient fire, the kiln may fire too quickly. Follow the rate of rise in temperature very carefully. If it is too fast, lower the fuel pressure and the air so that the firing is not over too soon.

2   *Clay and Clay Bodies*

Clay is a special material with unique properties. It is in itself formless, but it can be shaped into many forms. Although it is soft and pliable, it can be hardened by heat into one of the hardest materials known. To understand the nature of ceramics, the potter must understand the nature of clay.

Clays are composed of tiny particles of silica, alumina, and impurities. These particles occur in a way that gives clay its unique character. The particles take the form of flat platelets, so tiny they can be viewed only under the intense magnification of the electron microscope. When the platelets are suspended in water (approximately ⅔ dry clay and ⅓ water), each platelet slides along the surface of the next; this is what gives clay its workability. The total of many platelets forms a mass, which has much integrity yet can be shaped and modeled. Its workability is central to the nature of clay.

Wherever clays are found throughout the world, each deposit has a different character. Though all clays are composed of platelets of silica, alumina, and impurities, they differ greatly in the proportion of each material to the other and in the amount and types of the impurities they contain. They also vary in their particle size; some are comparatively coarse, and others are extremely fine.

Very early in the history of ceramics, potters learned how to modify clays by combining different clays or by adding nonclay materials such as sand or wood ashes to make their clays more workable, stronger, or otherwise more useful. These potters were making the first clay bodies. Contemporary potters almost always work with clay bodies which have become complicated mixtures of clay and nonclay materials. Nonclay materials are added to clay bodies to control plasticity, shrinkage, or warpage or to improve durability or color. It is not unusual to make up clay bodies containing three of four different clays and two or three nonclay materials. By balancing the characteristics of one material with another, the potter can tailor clay bodies to meet the specific requirements of firing temperature, workability, shrinkage, strength, and color.

Important Characteristics of Clay Bodies in Oxidation

1. *Firing temperature:* Oxidation clay bodies may be fired in a wide range of temperatures, ranging from a low of about cone 08 (945°C) to a high of about cone 14 (1390°C).

2. *Working characteristics* (often termed plasticity): This is generally the same for oxidation and reduction clay bodies. Other factors, such as maturation temperature and clay body types, have a far greater influence on working characteristics than does intended firing atmosphere.

3. *Color:* Oxidation clay bodies have a rather sober and reticent character compared to reduction.

4. *Texture:* Oxidation clay bodies generally do not have the rich visual texture of reduction bodies.

5. *Glaze* (body reactions): These reactions are much more obvious in reduction firing, with its strong texture of dark spots coming through the glaze from the clay body. Glaze color and tone, however, are profoundly affected by the clay body character in the oxidation fire.

Clay Body Categories

To understand the almost infinite variety of clay bodies available, it is useful to subdivide them into categories according to the ratio of clay to nonclay materials in the body formula. This ratio has an important impact on the character of the clay body.

Bodies that are high in clay and low in nonclay materials tend to be easy to work with, and their texture and color tend to be earthy and natural. Bodies that are comparatively low in clay and high in nonclay materials are much more difficult to work with; however, they offer a material with a rich, refined character.

It is possible, by careful manipulation, to devise a type of clay body that enjoys many of the best characteristics of both the high clay and the low clay formulations. These formulas, which are moderate in their clay to nonclay ratio, are especially well suited to the oxidation fire.

In low fire temperatures, high clay content bodies are generally called terra-cotta. In the high fire they are called stoneware. Medium clay content bodies go by names such as white bodies or porcelainous bodies. In this book I have chosen to use the term fineclay or fineclay body, a term in limited use but one that is useful and descriptive; this term is applied to both low- and high-fire medium clay bodies.

Low clay bodies in the low fire are called talc bodies, low fire porcelains, or soft paste bodies (a translation of the French phrase *pâté tendre*). In the firing range from cone 2 to cone 7, they are called porcelainous, porcelainlike, or porcelain-type bodies. In the high fire at cone 8 and above, these bodies are called porcelain.

CLAY BODY CATEGORY CHART

High clay bodies	*Medium clay bodies*	*Low clay bodies*
clay: 100–82%	clay: 80–62%	clay: 60–45%
nonclay: 0–18%	nonclay: 20–38%	nonclay: 40–55%

STONEWARE CLAY BODIES

Many of these clay bodies are somewhat coarse and may be considered as "workhorse" clay body types. Often substantial amounts of grog or sand are added to increase strength and coarseness.

Although white bodies with a high clay content are possible (especially at cone 9), most high clay bodies are made from clays with an iron content. Most are tans, gray, or brown.

FINECLAY BODIES

This term designates a kind of clay body with a moderate clay content. Although it may contain some rough-textured clays, fine-textured clays generally predominate in the formula. If carefully formulated, this kind of clay body may come close to stoneware in workability, but its character may be like that of the low clay bodies. Fineclays vary greatly in color, with off-whites, tans, soft grays, browns, and umbers common.

Fineclay bodies have a character that is especially appropriate to the oxidation fire. Just as the rough and natural effects of stoneware are effective in the reduction fire, the quieter and more reserved quality of fineclay bodies is especially well suited to oxidation.

PORCELAIN AND PORCELAIN-TYPE CLAY BODIES

It is necessary here to make a distinction between porcelain and porcelain-type clay bodies. It is difficult to define true porcelain, but most potters seem to agree that its two essential characteristics are whiteness and translucency. In

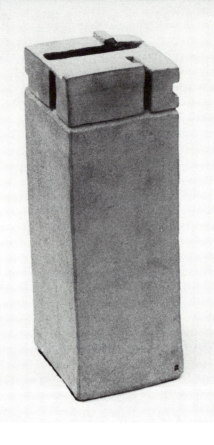

2-1   Richard Zakin. Oswego, New York. *Sculptural Form*. Cone 6. Handbuilt. Four percent Barnard clay was added to a normal, light tan oxidation body. The result is a soft, rich gray brown clay body that needs little or no added glaze.

2-2   Richard Zakin. Oswego, New York. *Modular Tile Piece*. Fired, unglazed, cream-colored clay. Because there is a strong pattern of light and shade in this piece, there was no need to use glaze or other coloring materials on the clay. In this case only the simplest surface treatment was appropriate.

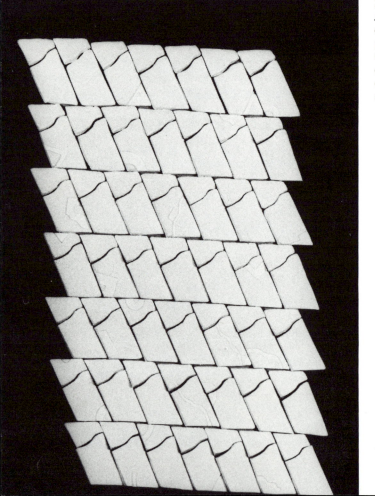

2-3   William Daley. Philadelphia, Pennsylvania. *Onega's Passage*. Cone 6. Handbuilt.
Daley uses the simple yet rich color and texture of oxidation-fired clay for these
massive vessels.

2-4   William Daley. Philadelphia, Pennsylvania. *Jonah II*. Cone 6.

2-5   William Daley. Philadelphia, Pennsylvania. *Toas Procession*. Cone 6.

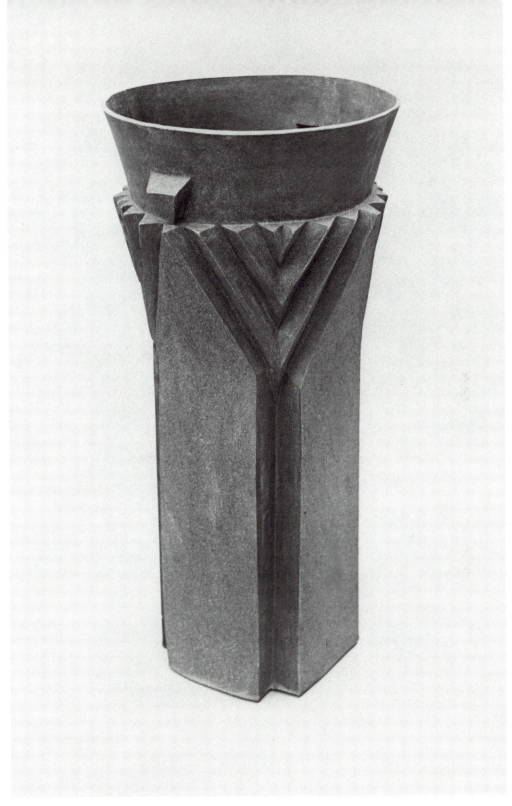

2-6 William Daley. Philadelphia, Pennsylvania. *Palmed Stuft*. Cone 6.

2-7   Dzintars Mezulis. Toronto,
Ontario. *The Repentant Fox.* Cone 6.
Handbuilt, unglazed stoneware
body. The complicated form works
well with the simple surface of the
unglazed stoneware.

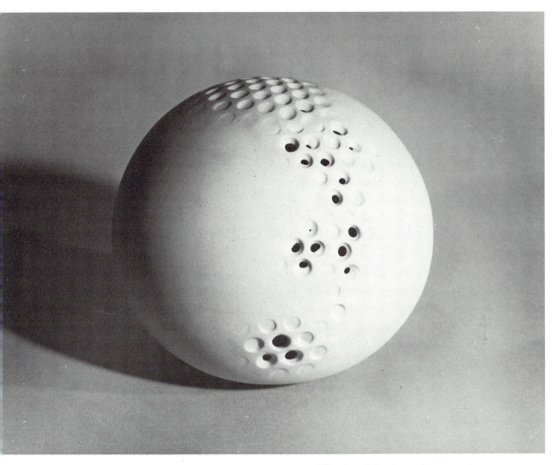

2-8 Ann Mortimer. Newmarket, Ontario. *Sculptural Piece.* Cone 9. Mold made, sand blasted. The rich surface of this piece is due to the unglazed clay body. Any glaze would have been superfluous.

practice most porcelain bodies are off-white and must be worked in fairly thin sections for their translucent character to show through. This is usually achieved by using a formula composed of 40 to 50 percent nonplastic materials, namely silica (flint) and flux; the rest is reserved for the clays. If a clay body has this formula but does not meet the dual requirements of whiteness and translucency, then it is usually termed a porcelain-type clay body. In this book I have chosen to abide by these definitions in most of my formulas; only a few are called porcelain.

Porcelain bodies work especially well when fired in the oxidation atmosphere. The characteristics of the material and the fire match each other closely. Porcelain is a brilliant material, and glazes look rich and vibrant over it. Great ceramic artists at the beginning of this century, such as Taxile Doat, Auguste Delaherche, and Adelaide Alsop Robineau, worked in oxidation-fired porcelain.

This clay body is very high in nonclay materials; the body is therefore nonplastic and difficult to work with. These difficulties are compensated for by a feeling of great refinement. Porcelain clay bodies are fine in texture and rich in body color and work well with glazes. Clays used in this body type should be fine or medium fine in texture. Nonclay materials, which take up 40 to 50 percent of the formula, are divided between flint and various fluxes.

Porcelain is generally used for small- and medium-scale work in sculpture and pottery. This is because porcelain and porcelain-type clay bodies, with their high nonclay content, do not have the plasticity and workability needed for large work. An experienced worker often will accept these risks, however, and, pushing to the limits of the material, work in a fairly large scale with these clay bodies. Involved and highly personal methods may be devised for coping with the limitations of the material, including adding plasticizers; using special ball clays, kaolins, or special fluxes; and using specialized forming methods.

Porcelain is equally challenging to the thrower and the hand builder. It lends itself to work of a controlled, classical character. At its best, it conveys a feeling of intelligence and purpose.

COLORED CLAY BODIES

Potters are much more concerned nowadays about hazards connected with ceramics than they were in the past. With this in mind it is important to take a long and careful look at colored clay techniques. Although potters use colorants all the time, it is easier to exercise prudence when glazing than it is when working with colored clay bodies.

It is arguable that potters should limit themselves to natural clays and clay bodies composed of naturally occurring clays. This would give them a limited palette of white, off-whites, tans, grays, browns, and umbers.

The clay body formulas listed in the formula section of this book are safe, and in many cases are compatible and should serve as a fine starting point for experiments in colored clay techniques.

2-9 Henry Lyman, Jr. Clinton,
New York. Cone 9. Lyman works in
porcelain, often fired in oxidation.
He is an admirer of both copper red
and copper blue, the former derived
from reduction, the latter from
oxidation.

2-10 Mary Rogers. Leicestershire, England. Approximately cone 10. Hand-modeled porcelain fired to 1300°C. Using stains, colorants, and glazes on the unfired porcelain clay body, Rogers achieves rich, dappled surfaces and translucent effects.

2-11 Mary Rogers. Leicestershire, England. Approximately cone 10. Hand-modeled porcelain, fired to 1300°C.

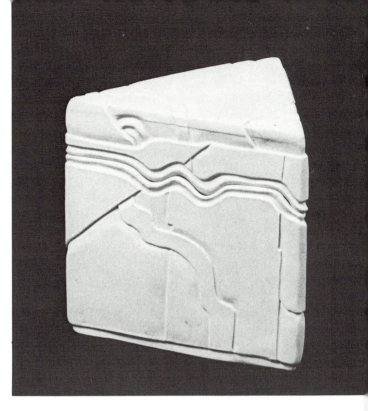

2-12   Richard Zakin. Oswego, New York.
Covered Jar. Cone 6. Handbuilt, carved,
white fineclay. This piece was glazed with
a clear, high-silica glaze (volcanic ash,
transparent base).

2-13   Elizabeth MacDonald. Brookfield,
Connecticut. *Vase.* Cone 7. Handbuilt.
MacDonald works with earth-colored and
white clay bodies. After bisque firing,
glaze is applied to the interstices. The
method is natural and direct.

2-14 Elizabeth MacDonald. Brookfield, Connecticut. Cone 7.

2-15 Elizabeth MacDonald. Brookfield, Connecticut. Cone 6. *Photo by Robert E. Barrett*

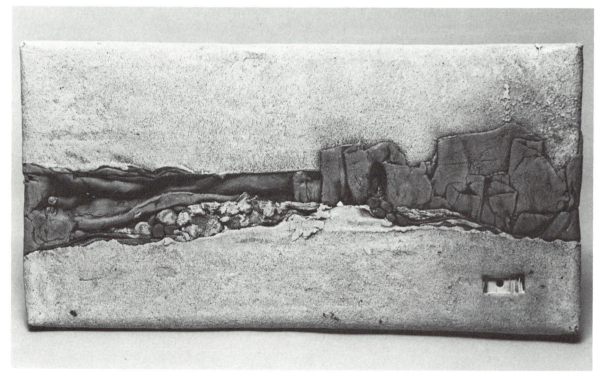

GRIT CLAY BODIES

Usually any grog or sand content in a clay body is listed separately from the clay body formula and is not considered a central element in the formula. Regardless of whether some grog or white sand is present or not, the formula is considered essentially unchanged.

In these grit clay bodies, however, with their high percentage of sand or grog, additions must be considered an integral part of the formula. These additions are not present in small amounts to control cracking and shrinking but rather in amounts sufficient to influence the look of the fired clay body. Large additions of sand or grog should be compensated for by the use of plastic clays in the clay part of the formula.

This sort of clay body can be of great interest to the oxidation potter, for it features a uniquely soft, rich surface. Grogs and sands of various colors, when added to clay bodies, produce a stony, granitelike look.

The ceramist will find these clay bodies appropriate for hand-formed work. They are acceptable only for the roughest sort of throwing and only to potters with tough hands.

BONE ASH FLUX WHITE CLAY BODIES

Bone ash (calcium phosphate) is a powerful body flux that encourages translucency. Unfortunately, it is highly alkaline; and clay bodies high in alkaline materials are low in workability. Bone ash therefore is not a suitable flux for the potter who works with hand-building or throwing methods. It is a good flux for slip cast work, however.

Clay Supplies

Many potters buy premixed clay from ceramic supply houses. It would be better if potters bought dry clay and mixed their own clay bodies; the product is much more uniform and reliable. Also, potters who mix their own bodies understand their work better. It is all too easy for a supplier to misweigh or substitute ingredients or to neglect such niceties as cleaning the mixing machinery. Problems can only be detected after the firing, and then it is often too late.

Many suppliers try to sell clay bodies that supposedly mature at a very wide range of temperatures. This would be a welcome innovation, but clay just does not work this way and it is not a good idea to pretend that it does. Clay bodies mature at a specific temperature. While some leeway can be allowed (perhaps 20°C above or below), too much is simply wishful thinking. Potters who buy premixed clay bodies should buy them from suppliers who are rigorous and specific in their approach.

Custom-made clay bodies that are made to order by a reliable supplier often have proved to be the best solution to the clay supply problem. In this case the potter needs a good source for the clay body formula before ordering

2-16 Marylyn Dintenfass. Mamaroneck, New York. Cone 3. Semi-mat nepheline glaze. Sculptural clay bodies are often fired to a point where they are hard but not mature (a sort of high-bisque fire). This piece was treated this way. The result is a clay body with little or no tendency to cracking or warping.

2-17 Marylyn Dintenfass. Mamaroneck, New York. Cone 9. Handbuilt, porcelain clays. These pieces show a natural appreciation for clay. They are finished simply and with elegant restraint. An opaque white glaze is used throughout.

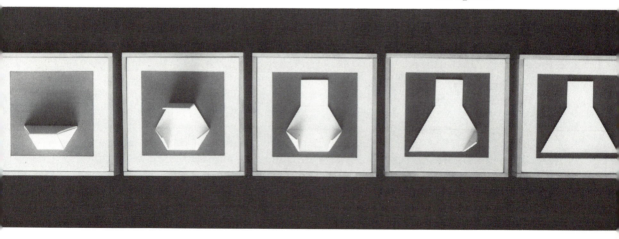

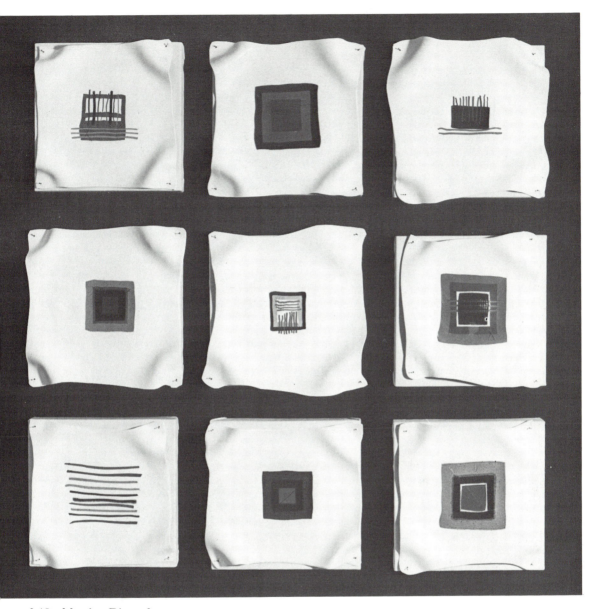

2-18 Marylyn Dintenfass.
Mamaroneck, New York.
Cone 3.

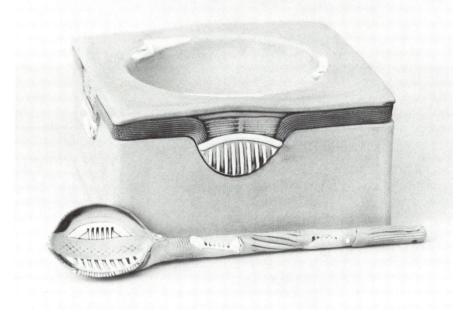

2-19 Katherine Dennison. *Decorative Bowl and Spoon*. Handbuilt with impressed decoration; colored clays, finished with glaze stains. In this piece and the one following, the impressed imagery is quite rich. Dennison found that only a light surface stain was necessary to finish the piece.

2-20 Katherine Dennison. *Covered Jars*. Cone 6. Handbuilt.

it in large quantity. (For many suppliers, the minimum order for a custom body is 1,000 pounds.) It is a simple procedure to make up a small amount of clay, perhaps 1,000 grams. It is usually a good idea to make up two or three formulas from a good source and then test them. The most suitable clay body then may be ordered from the supplier.

Making Clay Bodies

To make your own clay bodies you need a supply of dry clays. These are similar to glaze-making materials and are available at a ceramic supply house.

Weigh the materials and place them in a plastic bucket. Add enough water to make a thick pasty mixture; 40 percent water by weight is a good rule of thumb. Stir this first with a paddle and then, if possible, with a paint stirrer attached to a small power drill. This will ensure a smooth, well-mixed clay body.

The mixture now is too wet to be workable, although the excess water was necessary to good mixing. The clay now must be dried either on plaster or newspapers. Newspapers are preferable, as they are always available and they dry clay well. A thousand grams of clay can be dried in an hour or so. Spread the clay in a fairly thin layer over the newspaper, and then cover it with another layer of newspaper. (Try stacking alternating layers of newspaper and clay.) After a few minutes, when the clay has set a bit, place a board and a weight on top of the stack to squeeze the water out of the clay. You may speed up the process by trading dry newspaper for wet, although you cannot pull away the newspaper touching the clay until the clay is nearly dry; just change all the wet newspapers except those touching the clay.

When the clay is at working consistency, newspaper peels easily from it. Cut and wedge the clay thoroughly. Let it sit overnight, and it is ready to be worked.

You also may wish to mix up fairly large lots of your own clay body. Again, find a body formula that you like. Then order the dry clays from your supplier; they are available in 50- and 100-pound bags.

Weigh the clays (using a bucket and a bathroom scale) and put them in a plastic garbage container. Add 40 percent water (by weight) and stir with a paddle and, if possible, with a motor drill with a paint stirrer or clay mixer attached (the Jiffy Mixer is very good). Mix the clay well.

Use newspapers for drying the clay, alternating two-inch layers of clay and newspaper. To dry large lots of clay quickly, place weights on a board on top of the whole thing; this squeezes most of the water out of the clay. The whole process usually takes from 24 to 48 hours.

This is not the only method of making clay, nor is it the best; there is no one best method. It is a good method for making a hundred pounds or less of clay, and it is useful for the potter who uses that much in a week or two. (For the potter who goes through more than a hundred pounds of clay in a week, a clay mixer or pugmill is necessary.) The method outlined above has the advantages of economy, safety, and quietness, and it produces clay that is

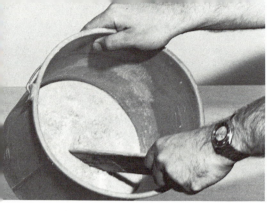

2-21   Stirring the dry clay body.

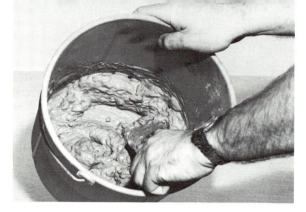

2-22   Adding enough water to the dry clay body to make a thick paste.

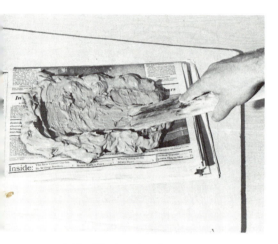

2-23   Placing the clay on newspapers (center is scooped).

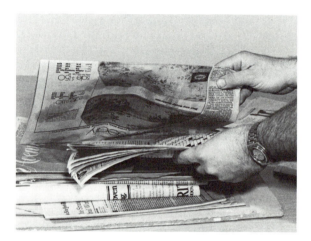

2-24   Piling up newspapers and clay.

2-25   The pile of newspapers and clay must "set" for a few minutes.

2-26   Placing a weight on the pile to speed drying.

2-27 Most of the moisture has
been absorbed by the newspapers.

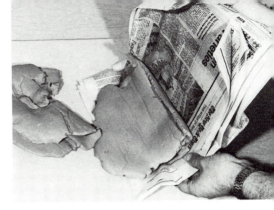

2-28 Releasing the clay slab.

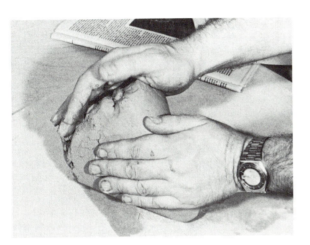

2-29 Wedging the clay.

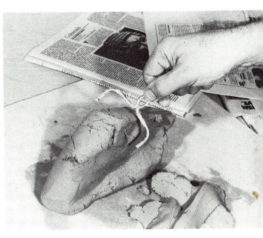

2-30 Using a cheese cutter to cut
the clay.

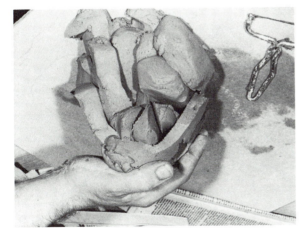

2-31 Packing and wedging the
clay.

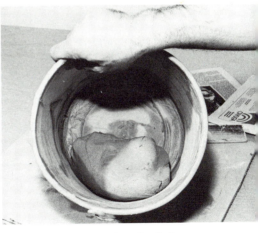

2-32 The completed wedged clay.

accommodating and plastic. Normally, freshly mixed clay must be stored for about three months to be as accommodating as clay produced by this wet method. Wet-mixed clay tends to be plastic because during the mixing stage it is saturated with water. Even when it is dried to a normal working consistency, the clay platelets are surrounded by water in a way that only aged mechanically-mixed clay can duplicate.

Testing Clay Bodies

You may wish to test various body and glaze formulas. It is not wise to test on finished objects. First test with test tiles. Illustrated below are test tiles for bodies and glazes that work well and are convenient to fire and store.

A test body tile is illustrated in Figure 2-33, about 0.5 centimeter thick, 4 centimeters wide, and 14 centimeters long. The tile must be made when the clay has the same amount of moisture required for clay used for hand building or throwing. A line 10 centimeters long is inscribed in the center of the tile, and a hole for hanging is put at the end. When the tile is fired, the line is measured again; the line will have shrunk, indicating the shrinkage of the clay body. The tile is fired while propped up on two pieces of refractory material (pieces of clay or broken kiln shelf). In this way the potter will know if the clay will slump in the fire. A little slumping is expected, but if the clay warps too much it will be difficult to work with.

Figure 2-34 shows a tile used in glaze testing. This kind of test tile should be fairly large—10 to 12 centimeters high—and curved in such a way as to stand in the kiln without support. The surface of the test tile should be similar to the surface of your work; one of the test tiles in the illustration is carved for this reason.

Pyrometric Cones

A pyrometric cone is made of ceramic material and designed to melt and slump at a given point in the firing, thus indicating the conditions inside the firing chamber. The potter needs to know about these conditions, but as the firing chamber is tightly closed and the atmosphere inside it is clouded and turbid from the action of heat and gases, this knowledge is hard to come by.

Pyrometric cones are narrow, three-sided pyramids. They are placed in front of a spy hole so they are clearly visible during the fire. When they mature, they soften and bend.

Pyrometric cones react to the conditions inside the firing chamber in much the same way that clays and glazes react. Although temperature influences those conditions, it is not the only factor. Others factors, such as kiln atmosphere and time, also affect the character of clay bodies and glazes. All these variables influence the action of the pyrometric cones, which is why they are such useful indicators of the conditions inside the kiln.

2-33   A test body tile.

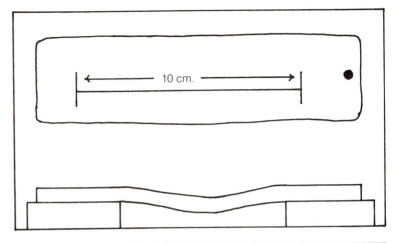

2-34   A glaze testing tile.

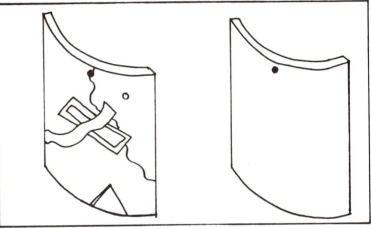

2-35   A test tile with throwing lines. This kind of tile is necessary for the potter whose work has throwing lines.

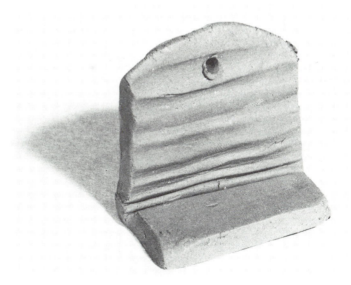

10 cm.

Most potters rely on the accuracy and consistency of pyrometric cones more than they rely on temperature indicators. This is so much the case that they refer to cones instead of temperature. Thus, for example, the term cone 3 is used instead of 1160°C. This system more accurately reflects conditions inside the firing chamber.

In this book I have chosen to work in three temperature ranges—cones 3, 6, and 9. Cone 3 is a midfire temperature (it bends at about 1160–70°C). Cone 6 is a fairly high temperature (1220–30°C). Cone 9 is a high temperature (1275–85°C).

Each category is valuable in one way or another, but each has drawbacks as well:

Cone 3. Color is a strong point of this firing range; the potter has a wide choice of strong saturated colors. Clay bodies, although fairly strong and workable, cause some problems. Glazes are good, but they must be formulated carefully and fluxed strongly. One consideration is economy, a strong argument in favor of cone 3.

Cone 6. Color still can be brilliant at cone 6 but not as brilliant as at cone 3. Clay bodies are often very workable. A wide variety of clay body types are possible; only true porcelain is unavailable at this temperature. Glazes have more leeway at cone 6 than at cone 3 as glazes need not be as strongly fluxed or carefully balanced.

Cone 9. Color is more muted than at cones 3 and 6. Clay bodies are tough and workable. True porcelain is the province of cones 9 and above. Glazes are rich and reliable. At cone 9, fluxes like calcium and magnesium come into their own; their usefulness at cone 6 is somewhat limited, and very limited at cone 3.

Cone 3 Clay Bodies

Cone 3 is a true midfire temperature. Although the lower and higher firing temperatures have been more popular in the past (perhaps because they have a more easily identifiable character), clay bodies in this temperature range offer important advantages; they are economical to fire, rich in color, and extremely durable.

Before I began to work extensively at cone 3, I assumed that darker clay bodies would be the most successful. After experimenting however, I have come to feel that cream-colored clay bodies are just as good or even better than the dark bodies fired at cone 3. Furthermore, light bodies may be used more readily with transparent and translucent glazes.

The cone 3 buff body given in the formula section is quite workable, with only a slight tendency to a "rubbery" feeling, but this is offset by a resistance to drying and firing cracks. Any of these bodies can benefit from the addition of white sand or grog, 2–6 percent, to make them more workable when wet and tougher during firing, to reduce heat distortion.

Bowerstown Dark Fine Clay

Cedar Heights Redart	40%	*With aging (two months or more) this body is strong and fairly workable. It is a rich medium brown.*
Cedar Heights Goldart	25	
Talc	15	
Ball clay	12	
Pine Lake fire clay	8	
White sand or grog	2	

Bainbridge Buff Fine Clay

Cedar Heights Goldart	52%	*This body is more workable than the Bowerstown body, although it feels slightly rubbery at times. Its color is very fine, it works well with all sorts of glazes, and it resists cracking.*
Ball clay	12	
Pine Lake fire clay	10	
Talc	22	
Potash feldspar	4	
White sand or grog	2	

Occanum Buff Fine Clay

Cedar Heights Goldart	48%	*A very tough, workable body. It is not as light in color as the Bainbridge body.*
Pine Lake fire clay	12	
Ball clay	12	
Talc	14	
Potash feldspar	14	

2-36 Jerry Caplan. Pittsburgh,
Pennsylvania. Cone 2. This
wonderful photograph shows fresh
sewer pipe, right at the factory,
transformed into a sculptural group.
The clay is an orange-burning, terra-
cotta color. The pieces were fired in
the plant's normal manner, cone 2
oxidation.

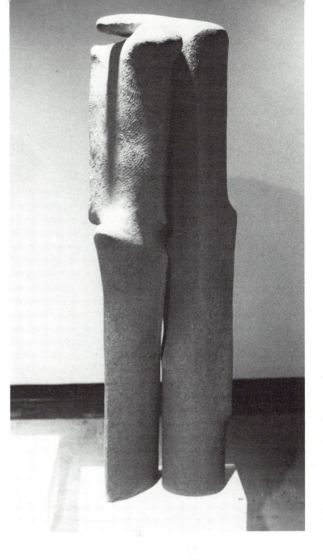

2-37   Jerry Caplan. Pittsburgh, Pennsylvania. Cone 2.

2-38   Mary Jane Moross. Chappaqua, New York. Cone 3/4. Moross's work is made with a clay body that fires at cone 3/4 to the equivalent of a high-bisque firing. In this way she insures that she can control cracking, warping, and shrinkage.

Cone 6 Clay Bodies

Cone 6 clay bodies offer the potter great advantages in terms of durability and workability. Only in the case of true porcelain is there any need to fire higher than cone 6. Cone 6 clay bodies may be made in a great variety of colors and tones, ranging from very light off-whites to deep browns and umbers.

STONEWARE CLAY BODIES

The following three formulas are comprised of 90 percent clay and 10 percent nonclay material.

Deep Red Stoneware Body

Cedar Heights Redart	45%	*This is a deep, brick red. It is not as*
Six Tile kaolin	33	*strong or as easily worked as the salmon*
Ball clay	12	*red body. Its color is quite rich. It is*
Flint	10	*appropriate for small sculpture and hand-built pottery.*

Orange Ochre Stoneware Body

Cedar Heights Goldart	70%	*This clay body has a pleasing orange-ochre*
Cedar Heights Redart	10	*tone. It would also do well with the*
P.B.X. fire clay	10	*addition of 5 or 10 percent common sand.*
Potspar	5	*This is a fine, all-purpose clay body for*
Flint	5	*pottery and sculpture.*

Salmon Red

Cedar Heights Goldart	40%	*This body is a rich, medium-toned salmon*
Six Tile kaolin	20	*color. It is smooth, plastic, easy to work*
Ball clay	5	*with, and resistent to warping and*
Cedar Heights Redart	25	*cracking. This is an all-purpose body.*
Flint	5	
Potspar	5	

PORCELAIN-TYPE CLAY BODIES

Cone 6 bodies, no matter what their clay to nonclay ratio, cannot be called true porcelain in its strict definition since the firing temperature is too low. Furthermore, reasonably plastic porcelain-type bodies fired at cone 6 tend to be only marginally translucent, and translucency is generally accepted as the hallmark of true porcelain.

It therefore seems expedient to fire oxidation porcelain at cones 9 or 10, and many potters do just that. There are, however, good reasons for staying with cone 6 and using modified porcelain bodies. The color range of cone 6 porcelain glazes is quite wide. At cone 6 oxidation, strong yellows and pinks are added to the normal porcelain color spectrum. Also, the comparatively low maturation temperature of cone 6 firing insures a long life for the kiln and, in electric kilns, for the Kanthal firing elements.

Because the white clays used in porcelain are very pure and refractory (not easily melted at cone 6), their formulas must contain strong fluxes, such as sodium, calcium, and magnesium. These nonclay materials inhibit workability in throwing or hand building. I have tried to solve these problems wherever possible.

Talc Body I
56% clay, 44% nonclay materials

Six Tile kaolin	24%	*This clay body has many of the workability*
Velvacast	24	*problems of porcelain-type bodies. Though not*
Flint	14	*very strong, it is quite plastic. Its fired color*
Potash feldspar	14	*is a rich, dense white. It is appropriate for*
Nepheline syenite	12	*small vessels and sculpture and can be used*
Ball clay	8	*by the throwing potter as well as the hand*
Talc	4	*builder.*
Macaloid	1.0	
Bentonite	0.5	

Talc Body II
56% clay, 44% nonclay materials

Six Tile kaolin	30%	*This body is very similar to Talc Body I in*
Velvacast	18	*both formula and character. It too is*
Flint	18	*appropriate for small vessels and sculpture.*
Nepheline syenite	12	*It can be used by the throwing potter and the*
Potash feldspar	8	*hand builder.*
Ball clay	8	
Talc	6	
Macaloid	1.0	
Bentonite	0.5	

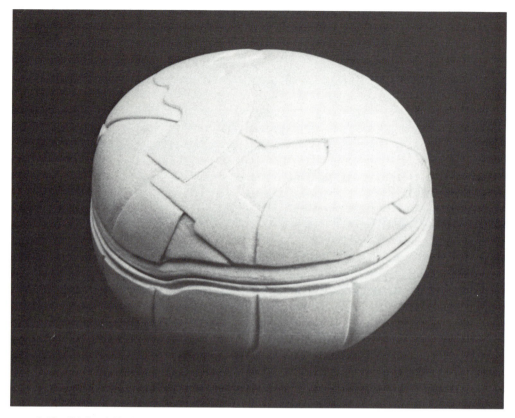

2-39 Richard Zakin. Oswego, New
York. Cone 6. Porcelainous body,
unglazed. Because this piece was
highly carved, it did not need (or
want) glaze.

Boron Porcelainous Fineclay

50% clay, 50% nonclay materials

Six Tile kaolin	22%	*This body is a rich, dense, translucent*
Velvacast	22	*white. The potter must pay a price for*
Ball clay	6	*translucency at cones 5 to 7; this body is*
Potash feldspar	26	*not very workable. It is appropriate for*
Flint	16	*small scale work.*
Frit 90 or 3124	8	
Macaloid	1.0	
Bentonite	0.5	

Dolomite Porcelainous Fineclay

55% clay, 45% nonclay materials

Six Tile kaolin	30%	*This clay body is a brilliant, opaque*
Velvacast	18	*white. It is very rugged, and for a body*
Ball clay	7	*with this much nonclay material, it is very*
Flint	16	*workable. Size considerations still apply*
Nepheline syenite	14	*but less so than with more translucent*
Potash feldspar	7	*bodies such as the Talc bodies and the*
Dolomite	8	*Boron body. It is appropriate for*
Macaloid	1.0	*throwing and hand building.*
Bentonite	0.5	

2-40 Richard Zakin. Oswego, New York. *Vase.* Handbuilt, carved and pierced; porcelain type white clay and opaque white glaze. The soft-looking ivory white body is finished with a glaze of the same character.

2-41 Rudolf Staffel. Philadelphia, Pennsylvania. Approximately cone 5. Staffel has
developed a uniquely personal approach to porcelain. Though his pieces resemble
normal container forms, they are meant to contain only light. Staffel goes to the
greatest lengths to achieve translucency. His clay bodies contain very little clay; they
are mostly formulated with nonclay materials (usually 70 percent or more of the body
is composed of nonclay materials). This type of body formula encourages
translucency. These bodies are difficult to work with and difficult to fire. Staffel
carefully watches the ware in the kiln toward the end of the firing. When the pieces
begin to distort, he terminates the firing. This way he gets as much translucency as
possible from his clay.

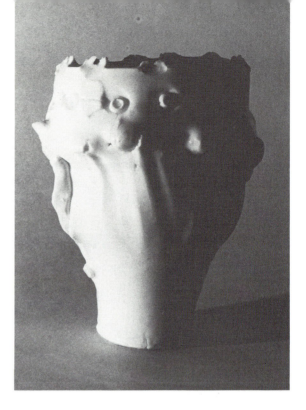

2-42　Rudolf Staffel.
Philadelphia, Pennsylvania.
Approximately cone 5.
*Courtesy of the Everson Museum,
Syracuse, N.Y.*

2-43　Rudolf Staffel. Philadelphia, Pennsylvania. Approximately cone 5.

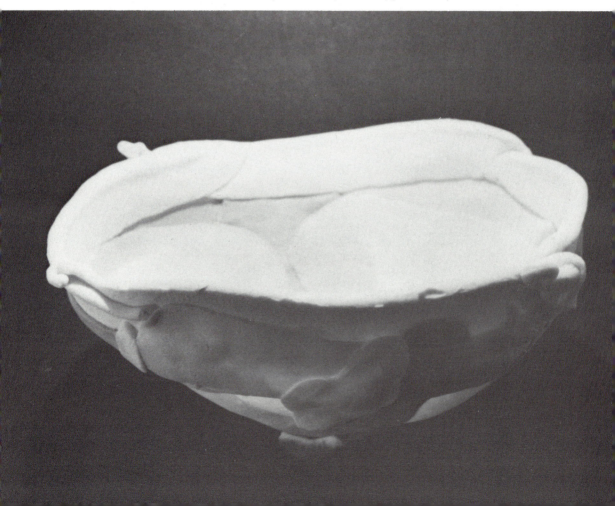

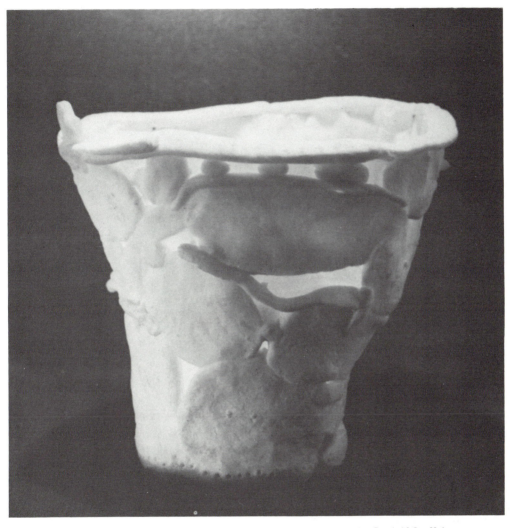

2-44 Rudolf Staffel.
Philadelphia, Pennsylvania.
Approximately cone 5.

GRAY WHITE PORCELAIN FINECLAY BODIES

These bodies are interesting because, though they follow the classic porcelain formula in their clay to nonclay ratios, they deviate from that formula in materials, for they have a nonkaolin clay content. This gives these bodies workability and strength, qualities normally not associated with porcelain body formulas.

October Body

56% clay, 44% nonclay materials

Cedar Heights Goldart	48%	*The high percentage of stoneware clay in*
Ball clay	8	*this formula lends plasticity and good*
Potash feldspar	12	*working qualities to the body. It is a*
Nepheline syenite	10	*pleasant ivory color.*
Flint	18	*The potter should be able to work in a*
Dolomite	4	*fairly large scale with this body.*
		It is suitable for throwing and hand
		building.

September V A

50% clay, 50% nonclay materials

Ball clay	8%	*The small percentage of Pine Lake fire*
Six Tile kaolin	34	*clay in this formula gives the body tooth,*
Pine Lake fire clay	8	*strength, and a particle size variety, the*
Flint	23	*key to good workability. Pine Lake is quite*
Potash feldspar	18	*mature at cone 6. Its presence in the*
Nepheline syenite	9	*formula enables the potter to use a great*
		deal of potash feldspar, which is less
		injurious to plasticity than strong fluxes
		like nepheline syenite. The body is a light
		oyster color, very strong with good
		workability. Pine Lake is a high-silica fire
		clay; do not attempt to replace it in the
		formula with a low-silica fire clay; the
		results will be poor.

Mathias Osterman. Toronto, Ontario. Cone 9. Sgraffitto has been used by oxidation potters in many places, among them China and Iran. Mathias Osterman uses the technique with fluidity and grace.

Emmanuel Cooper. London, England. *Thrown Bowl*. 1260° C (approximately cone 10). Emmanuel Cooper is an enthusiastic experimenter with oxidation fired glazes. Here he has used a uranium glaze.

Richard Zakin. Oswego, New York. August II body. Cone 6. Thin Mouse Black was daubed in the interstices. Corinth was then sprayed overall, and Brutus Blue was sprayed in localized areas.

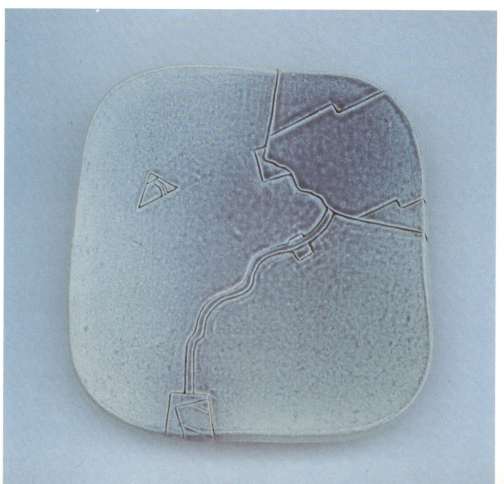

Dorothy Hafner. New York, New York. *Confetti*. Cone 6. Dorothy Hafner works with underglaze decoration. The oxidation fire is especially appropriate for graphic imagery of this type.

Val Barry. London, England. *Handbuilt Vases*. Cone 9. Val Barry's quiet, reserved pieces use soft, rich glazes with none of the harshness that is sometimes associated with the oxidation fire.

Jeanne McRight. Stirling, Ontario. Cone 6. This porcelain box displays a rarified, individual character.

Mary Rogers. Leicestershire, England. Cone 9. Mary Rogers uses both stains and glazes to achieve images of great delicacy.

Karl Martz. Bloomington, Indiana. Cone 3. Karl Martz has been making these severe and beautiful oxidation glazed pots for a number of years. Above fashion and bandwagon psychology he has chosen to explore an area that has had importance for him. These pieces are persuasive and thoughtful. *Collection of Rosemary and Dean Fraser.*

John Chalke. Calgary, Alberta. Cone 6. John Chalke's graphic imagery results from the multiple use of glazes, slips, stains, and colored clays. Here he has used stains and glazes together.

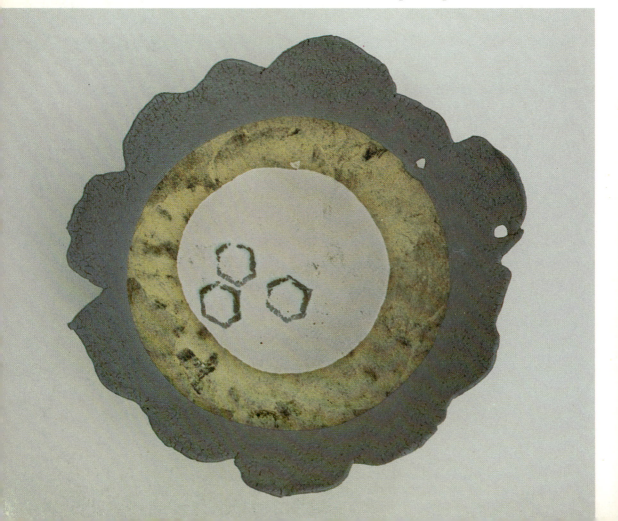

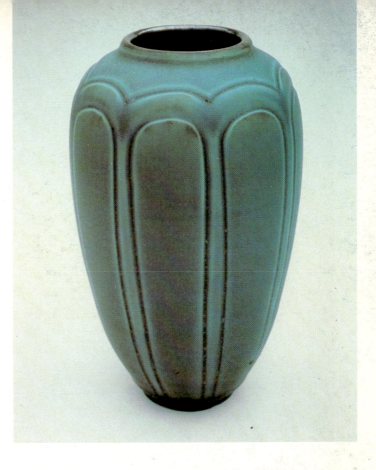

Phyllis Ihrman. Detroit, Michigan. *Thrown Vase.* Cone 9. Phyllis Ihrman always works with single fired porcelain in the oxidation fire. Great attention is paid to detail which, through hard work, is made to look quite effortless.

Edwin and Mary Scheier. Green Valley, Arizona. Cone 8/9. This beautiful piece is a fine example of Edwin and Mary Scheier's linear drawing style.

Richard Zakin. Oswego, New York. Cone 6. The blue glaze (Wollastonite III base plus cobalt) was brushed on the platter after Mouse Black was daubed in the interstices. The piece was then dipped in a clear wood ash glaze and fired to cone 6.

Tony Hepburn. Alfred, New York. *Cup Element.* Cone 9. Tony Hepburn uses glazed and unglazed clay in his pieces, and much of his work involves colored clay bodies.

Henry Lyman, Jr. Clinton, New York. Cone 9. Henry Lyman works in porcelain to obtain a graphic antique quality.

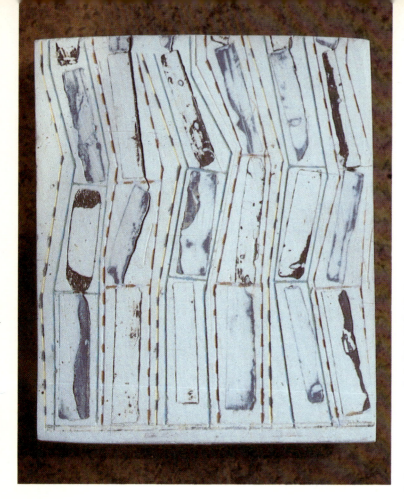

William Hall. High Wycombe, Buckinghamshire, England. *Handbuilt Plaque.* Cone 9. William Hall works on tiles and plaques with a variety of oxidation techniques, including the intensive use of slips and stains. Many of his pieces undergo multiple firings.

Eileen Nisbet. *Horizontal Flower.* 1240° C (approximately cone 9). Eileen Nisbet works in wafer-thin sheets of porcelain, which she assembles after firing. *Photo courtesy Pitman House Limited.*

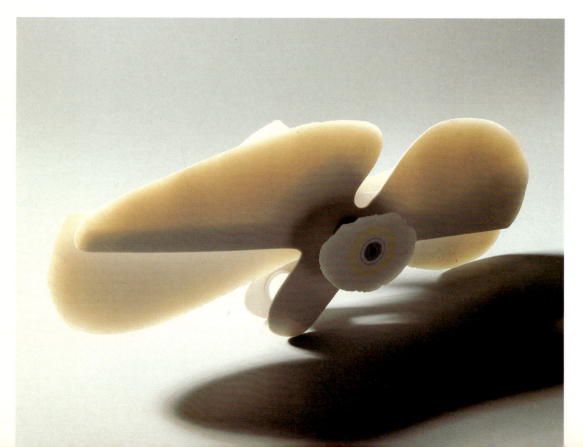

Mutsuo Yanagihara. Kyoto, Japan. *Memory of Sky I.* Cone 9. We tend to associate this sort of work with the low fire; however, it is very appropriate to high fire oxidation as well. Furthermore, many potters wish to work with the durable clays and glazes of the higher fire.

Richard Zakin. Oswego, New York.
August II body. Cone 6. A thin
Mouse Black was daubed in the
interstices. K 15 was sprayed overall,
and Burlington with cobalt and iron
was sprayed at the top.

Richard Zakin. Oswego, New York.
U.B.I. body. Cone 6. This piece was
sprayed with G.K. white glaze.
Brutus base with 2 percent
manganese dioxide was sprayed over
the shoulder and top.

Richard Zakin. Oswego, New York.
Cone 6. A white gritty slip was
applied to the clay, then the piece
was fired to bisque. Bistre stain was
daubed in the interstices and the
piece fired to maturity.

Marylyn Dintenfass. Mamaroneck,
New York. *Color Study #1.* Cone 9.
The sculptural qualities of this wall
hanging piece are emphasized by the
simple glaze surface.

Wayne Cardinelli. Stirling, Ontario. Cone 6. Wayne Cardinelli works in wood ash glazes in the electric kiln, obtaining results reminiscent of salt glazes.

Harry Horlock Stringer. London, England. A two glaze application procedure is used to create this rich warm tone.

William Hunt, Columbus, Ohio. William Hunt's glazes come from intuitive mixtures rather than formulas. In the hands of an expert, this method results in rich, warm colors and a wide range of textures.

Eileen Lewenstein. Sussex, England. Cone 9. Eileen Lewenstein is an expert at obtaining rich visual effects from the oxidation fire. These simple shapes are enhanced by the texture of their glazes.

Wayne Bates. Murray, Kentucky. Cone 6. Wayne Bates' work has a crisp graphic quality and an ethereal sense of color.

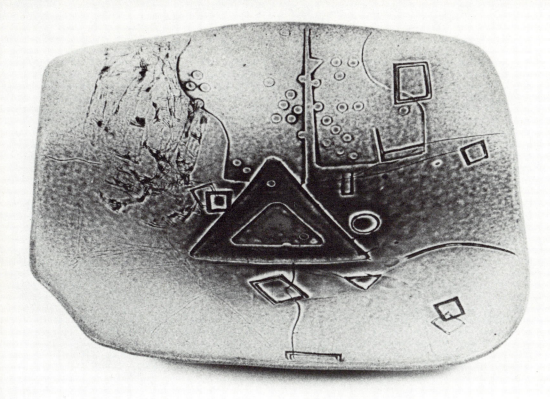

2-45   Richard Zakin. Oswego, New York.
Platter. Handbuilt with impressed imagery;
white fineclay with sprayed, modulated
glazes. In this piece the glaze color is
enhanced by the white color of the clay
underneath. A darker clay would have
darkened and grayed the glaze color.

2-46   Richard Zakin. Oswego, New York.
Cone 6. Another example of a piece made
with a white porcelainous fineclay, which
enhances the brilliance of the glaze.

WHITE FINECLAY BODIES

These bodies compared to white porcelain bodies work very well, are strong, and combine well with glazes. They have a much higher percentage of clay than do porcelain bodies, which gives them excellent working characteristics.

These bodies are very light in color. Although they do not have the light-gathering qualities of porcelain, their texture is smooth and rich.

The formulas shown below rely in part on the high silica content of Pine Lake fire clay. If this fire clay is unavailable in your area, do not substitute with a low-silica fire clay. Because Pine Lake fire clay is high in silica (64 percent), it has been used to compensate for the low silica content of the kaolin clays in these bodies.

U.B. I White Fineclay

75% clay, 25% nonclay

Ball clay	15%	*This is a fine, all-purpose clay body. It is*
Pine Lake fire clay	15	*easy to work and fairly strong. In overall*
Six Tile kaolin	45	*character it is not dissimilar to porcelain,*
Potash feldspar	20	*but it is much easier to work with. It is a*
Flint	5	*very light oyster gray.*

U.B. II Cream White Fineclay

75% clay, 25% nonclay

Cedar Heights Goldart	10%	*U.B. II is cream white. It is a very strong*
Ball clay	15	*and useful body. It differs from the U.B.*
Pine Lake fire clay	15	*I body formula only in its Goldart*
Six Tile kaolin	45	*stoneware clay content. It is more yellow*
Potash feldspar	20	*in color than U.B. I, but it is also*
Flint	5	*stronger and easier to use. It is a fine,*
		all-purpose body.

September V A White Fineclay

70% clay, 30% nonclay

Ball clay	12%	*This clay body does not have the*
Pine Lake fire clay	14	*workability characteristics of the U.B.*
Six Tile kaolin	44	*bodies. It is, however, very dense and*
Nepheline syenite	6	*white and has a porcelainlike character.*
Potash feldspar	12	
Flint	12	

January Body
85% clay, 15% nonclay materials

Cedar Heights Goldart	65%	*This clay body is comparatively high in clay and low in nonclay materials, which accounts in part for its workability. It is straw-colored and compatible with most glazes.*
Pine Lake fire clay	10	
Ball clay	10	
Potash feldspar	8	
Flint	4	
Talc	3	

FINECLAY BODIES

Dark Fineclay—Red Brown
75% clay, 25% nonclay materials

Cedar Heights Goldart	28%	*This is a very dense, smooth clay body. Its color is a curious cool gray-brown. It is quite workable and strong. Its deep color has a strong effect on glazes; it is at its best when used with very opaque glazes.*
Cedar Heights Redart	24	
Ball clay	14	
Six Tile kaolin	9	
Flint	14	
Potash feldspar	11	

August I Body
75% clay, 25% nonclay materials

Cedar Heights Goldart	55%	*This is a fairly plastic body with very good workability and great strength. Its color is a clear, straw yellow.*
Pine Lake fire clay	10	
Cedar Heights Redart	5	
Ball clay	5	
Potash feldspar	14	
Flint	11	

August II Clay Body
72% clay, 28% nonclay materials

Cedar Heights Goldart	54%	*This fineclay is similar to August I, except for its lighter color.*
Pine Lake fire clay	10	
Ball clay	8	
Potash feldspar	14	
Flint	12	
Talc	2	

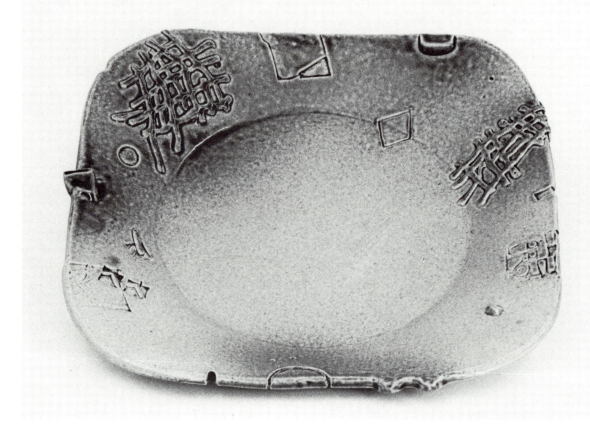

2-47 Richard Zakin. Oswego, New York. Cone 6. This piece was made with the U.B. I body, a white fineclay.

2-48 Richard Zakin. Oswego, New York. Cone 6. This piece was made with dark red-brown fineclay.

2-49   Dzintars Mezulis. Toronto, Ontario. *Uncle Zam Wants You*. Cone 6. Handbuilt.
In this piece, with its dark-colored clay body, the potter used glaze only as a local
accent. The result is a surface quality that emphasizes form rather than descriptive
color.

2-50 Dzintars Mezulis. Toronto, Ontario. *Dolmen Obscura*. Handbuilt. This is an unglazed dark-bodied piece with much emphasis on the strong textural surface.

2-51 John Chalke. Calgary, Alberta. *Platter*. Handbuilt; earth-colored clays. The
rich tonalities and textures of this piece are derived from the use of contrasting
ironbearing and non-ironbearing clays.

GRIT CLAY BODIES

Hampton Grit Clay Body I
56% clay, 44% nonclay

Ball clay	56%	*This clay body is very white, with a soft*
Potash feldspar	14	*pebbly texture like a sand dollar.*
Nepheline syenite	12	
Talc	4	
Flint	14	
+ White sand	40–60%	

Hampton Grit Clay Body II

Ball clay	40%	*This is similar to Hampton Grit Clay*
Cedar Heights Goldart	8	*Body I, though it is a little easier to use*
Pine Lake fire clay	8	*since the Goldart stoneware clay and the*
Nepheline syenite	12	*Pine Lake fire clay contribute toughness*
Potash feldspar	14	*and plasticity. The color is not as white.*
Talc	4	
Flint	14	
+ White sand	40–60%	

BONE ASH FLUXED CLAY BODIES

Handbuilding and Throwing Body

Six Tile kaolin	30%	*Because bone ash is a strong deflocculant,*
Velvacast	10	*this clay body is somewhat rubbery and*
Ball clay	10	*difficult to use. It is useful for small*
Flint	20	*work.*
Nepheline syenite	15	
Dolomite	5	
Frit 3124 (or 90)	5	
Bone ash	5	

Slipcast Body I

E.P.K. kaolin	40%	*With the addition of suitable deflocculants,*
Velvacast	10	*both this formula and the next are*
Flint	20	*excellent casting bodies.*
Soda spar	20	
Bone ash	10	

Slipcast Body II

E.P.K. kaolin	40%
Velvacast	10
Flint	20
Nepheline syenite	15
Frit 3124 (or 90)	10
Bone ash	5

2-52 Glenys Barton. London, England. *Sculptural Piece*. Barton works with slip-cast porcelains and bone china clay bodies. The imagery is crisp and controlled. It is served well by her technical approach.

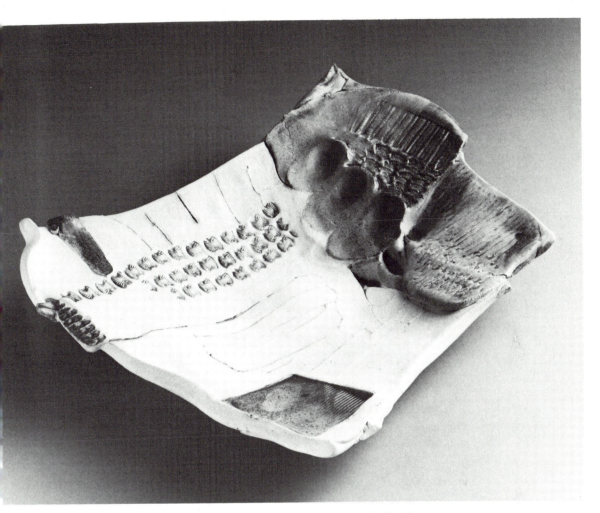

2-53   Louise Baldinger.
Schenectady, New York. Cone 9.
Baldinger produces pieces with
direct, graphic imagery. There is a
strong dialogue between the clay
surface and the glaze imagery. *Photo
by Richard Baldinger*

Cone 9 Clay Bodies

This is the part of the high-fire range that offers the potter the greatest strength in clay bodies and glazes. Clay bodies fired to this temperature range, because they are low in fluxes, can be very plastic and workable.

Although the firings at this temperature range are not as economical as those fired from cones 5 to 7, most electric kilns of good quality can easily achieve these temperatures. Coil life may be shortened somewhat, but as long as the elements are kept clean, this is not a problem.

Though the color range is narrower than at cone 6, the fired results are resonant and harmonious, perhaps more so than at cones 3 and 6.

PORCELAIN BODIES

Many potters who fire porcelain in oxidation fire at cones 9 and 10. Clay bodies for this temperature (1280°C) are strong and easily worked, and glazes tend to be soft and muted.

Classical formulations for porcelain bodies work very well at cones 9 and 10; these bodies are usually fluxed with potash feldspar, which is comparatively mild. Bodies containing this flux are fairly plastic.

Porcelain I

50% clay, 50% nonclay materials

Six Tile kaolin	30%	*This is a classical porcelain formula with two small variations. A small percentage of dolomite is added to the body formula; it is useful as a supplemental flux, and its bleaching action ensures a very white body. Two different kaolins are used: a smooth particled kaolin and a rough one. In this way a particle size variation is achieved, an important component of workability. Dense white and translucent, this body has good workability and is appropriate for throwing and hand building.*
Velvacast	14	
Ball clay	6	
Flint	25	
Potash feldspar	22	
Dolomite	3	

Porcelain II
50% clay, 50% nonclay

Six Tile kaolin	35%	*This clay body also uses two different*
Velvacast	8	*kaolins for particle size variation. Dense*
Ball clay	7	*white, with good strength and workability,*
Flint	23	*it is a fine, all-purpose porcelain body.*
Potash feldspar	27	

Porcelain III
50% clay, 50% nonclay

Six Tile kaolin	30%	*The talc content is an aid to plasticity and*
Velvacast	14	*crack resistance and helps make this body*
Ball clay	6	*very easy to work with.*
Flint	24	
Potash feldspar	22	
Talc	4	

STONEWARE BODY

Garratsville Body
92% clay, 8% nonclay

Cedar Heights Goldart	44%	*This clay body, with its unusual mixture*
Kaolin	20	*of kaolin and Goldart, is appealing for a*
Ball clay	14	*number of reasons: it is very workable, its*
Pine Lake fire clay	14	*texture is very fine, its color is cool gray,*
Dolomite	8	*and its character is refined. Most*
		important, this clay body works very well
		with cone 9 textured glazes. Textured
		glazes do well with porcelain bodies, but
		they are especially rich when sprayed over
		a darker body like this one.

2-54   Richard Zakin. Oswego, New York. *Two Wall Hanging Vases.* Cone 9. Handbuilt, carved and pierced porcelain body, clear glaze. In these pieces a simple clear glaze goes well with the character of porcelain clay, with its very hard, smooth surface and white color.

2-55   Richard Zakin. Oswego, New York. Cone 9. Porcelain.

2-56 Mary Rogers. Leicestershire, England. 1300°C. Hand-modeled porcelain. Cone 9 and 10 clay bodies can be quite fluid and workable. This piece demonstrates the kind of form an expert ceramist can produce with a good porcelain clay body.

2-57 Mary Rogers. Leicestershire, England. 1300°C. Hand-modeled porcelain, unglazed. Emphasis here is on the translucency that can be obtained using thin-walled porcelain clay bodies.

2-58 Eileen Nisbet.
Sculptural Piece. Cone 9.
Handbuilt, assembled. Nisbet
makes the most of the purity
and lightness characteristic of
porcelain fired in oxidation.

3   *Glazes*

If ceramics comprised only the art of making objects from clay, which then may be fired and made permanent, it still would hold a great fascination. There is more than clay, however, for a surface may be applied to modify all or part of the clay object. The potter has a very wide variety of choices among various sorts of surface finishes in terms of character, color, and visual and physical texture.

Glazes are a kind of glass, in many ways similar to common window glass. Glazes, however, are not meant to fit in a frame, as is window glass, but rather meant to fit over a frame, that frame being the form of the clay object. Glazes are the most commonly used finishing surface in ceramics; they offer the potter the option of a wide variety of visual effects—many of great beauty—along with the virtues of durability and usefulness.

Glaze Formulas

In certain types of ceramics, mainly low-fire hobby ceramics, the potter may purchase containers of premixed glazes. Some commercially available mixtures are formulated for the oxidation high-fire worker as well. Generally, however, potters mix glazes from formulas, made from about twenty materials commonly used by potters. Occasionally, students of ceramic technology combine some of these materials in a different way, and a successful new formula will result; few new formulas, however, are completely successful.

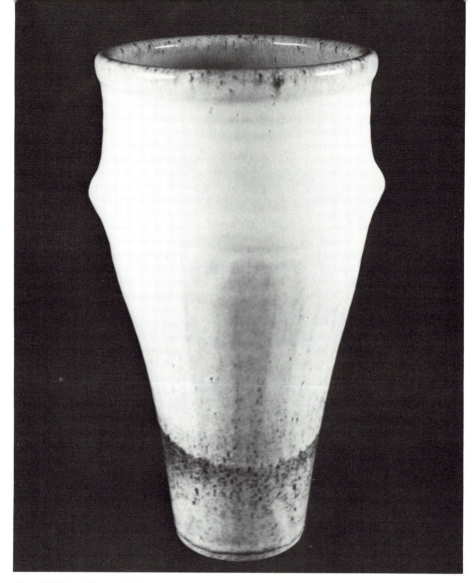

3-1 William Hunt. Columbus, Ohio. Hunt says of his work: "My oxidation glazes are all formulated intuitively in batches of up to 25 gallons, according to what I have learned over the years about various glaze ingredients. I employ a mix of local materials (even dirt from my back yard) and processed compounds from the glaze supplier, grocery, and drugstore. The initial glaze batch may have 17 to 20 ingredients. Then I test the glaze by firing and adjust its contents according to what seems required. The adjustments are all made by weighed additions with thorough records so that additional adjustments can be made with better knowledge of their potential reaction in the initial batch. The limitation and excitement of this method are that once a handsome or special glaze is found, it exists only in limited supply. The advantage of the system is that one need not settle for a mediocre or ordinary glaze but can add to the batch indefinitely until a suitable result is obtained. When occasionally the glaze tests look like they are going nowhere, the batch can be divided and major quantities of intuitive additions added to begin two new glazes from one problematic one. Sometimes I will even drastically change firing temperature in order to fully exploit a particular recipe, making objects specifically for that glaze, and firing a few kiln loads of nothing but that glaze until it is all used up."

Glaze formulas are much valued by potters, who take great pains to find new and different ones that will expand the range and enhance the beauty of their work.

Glaze Makeup

All stoneware and porcelain glazes contain alumina, silica, and flux (a melter). They are formulated so that they become glasslike when fired to a specific cone or temperature range. These glasslike surfaces are devised carefully to bond well with clay, to color and decorate the form, and to serve as a useful and strong surface for the form. In addition to silica, alumina, and flux, colorants or materials that render the glaze opaque (opacifiers) often are added to the glaze.

There is much similarity between the clay and glaze components. Clay bodies contain alumina, silica, and flux, as do glazes; this similarity insures that the bond between clay and glaze is very strong. Glazes, however, contain more flux than do most clay bodies and much more of the stronger fluxes.

There are myriad glaze formulas, each producing a different, unique result. Many formulas are, for one reason or another, unsuitable; some are unstable, some dull, some too soft, and others too runny. There are still many that make fine glazes and have much to offer the potter.

Glaze Character

Glazes take on many guises and have widely differing characters. Because of their wide variations, it is helpful to group glazes into broad types or categories, determined by the following criteria: light transmission, durability, and texture.

LIGHT TRANSMISSION

One way to identify glaze formulas is by light transmission. A transparent glaze is clear, transmitting light completely; translucent glazes transmit light, but they are cloudy; opaque glazes transmit little (if any) light. Translucent glazes, like opaque glazes, offer the possibility of soft modulated surfaces, but they disclose more of the clay body underneath the surface. Like transparent glazes, they pool where they are thick, especially if they are colored, which emphasizes surface imagery naturally.

Transparent glazes are clear, shiny and hard. They may be colorless or stained with color.

The best transparent glazes are high in silica and low in alumina. A high flux content is one way to produce a clear glaze, but high flux glazes generally are very weak. The best transparent glazes contain comparatively little flux. Although the percentage of flux is low, the power of the flux is high.

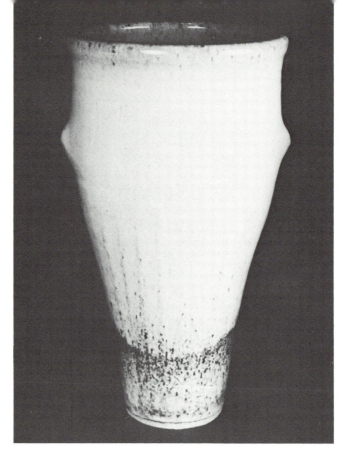

3-2 William Hunt.
Columbus, Ohio. Cone 6.

3-3 William Hunt.
Columbus, Ohio.

3-4   William Hunt. Columbus, Ohio.

Transparent glazes are used best on simple forms with smooth, unbroken surfaces. Almost all transparent glazes are shiny and reflect light easily. Active surfaces catch the light in complicated ways when finished with transparent glazes. Smooth, simple surfaces, on the other hand, are enriched by the depth and luxurious character of transparent glazes.

Because transparent glazes are among the strongest and most practical glaze types, they are often used on pieces intended for table use. In oxidation-fired ceramics, transparent glazes are especially luxurious when applied to white and porcelainous bodies, for they set off the pure character of the white body.

Translucent glazes transmit light incompletely. Many of the richest glazes in ceramics are translucent, such as celadon glaze and the milky white glaze that the Chinese used on porcelains.

Translucent glazes need not be as high in silica as transparent glazes. They tend to have a fairly high alumina and flux content.

Translucent glazes are used both for pottery and sculpture. They can be very smooth, making them appropriate for table pieces. Their pleasing character is not troubled by the multiple reflections of transparent glazes; they are therefore suitable for use on highly articulated surfaces. They are especially rich over light-colored bodies.

Opaque glazes transmit little or no light. Such ancient glazes as majolica and Tzu Chou, as well as many well-known modern glazes such as Mamo Mat, Woo Yellow, and Shaner Red, are opaque.

Glazes are rendered opaque by additions of alumina (usually clay) or opacifying materials, such as barium carbonate, tin oxide, or any one of a number of zirconium compounds. All of these materials interfere with the passage of light through the glaze, causing opacity.

Opaque glazes are usually low in flint and high in clay. Barium and the zirconium compounds modulate glaze surfaces to produce rich visual textures.

Opaque glazes are appropriate for many different types of work. Opaque glazes may be shiny and glasslike, making them especially useful where strength and practicality are required. Satin mats and mat opaque glazes have a rich, soft, claylike character that makes them valuable in sculpture and pottery. Mat opaque glazes do not reflect much light; they are appropriate for highly manipulated forms, where shiny glazes would be confusing.

DURABILITY

Glazes vary greatly in their resistance to scratches, abrasions, crazing, and flaking, which can be an important consideration in choosing a glaze. Glazes derive strength from alumina and silica; a few fluxes also contribute to wear resistance. Unfortunately, many fluxes that encourage a rich character also encourage soft, easily worn surfaces. Beauty occasionally must be sacrificed for usefulness, and vice versa. Strength is considered more important in pieces intended for the table than for other ceramic work.

3-5 Shirley Woodcock. Oswego, New York. Cone 6. This piece is made with a porcelain body (Talc I). The Mouse Black glaze was applied in the interstices, and the piece was covered with Volcanic Ash Clear glaze. The piece is very small, about the size of a golf ball, with a metal fitting in the bottom, which is threaded. It is an automobile gearshift knob.

3-6 Shirley Woodcock. Oswego, New York. Cone 6. This piece, a toothbrush holder, was daubed with Mouse Black in the interstices and covered with Volcanic Ash Clear glaze.

TEXTURE

Glazes vary in their "hand"—that is, the feel of their surface. Some glazes are smooth and glassy, others dry and stony. Potters use the terms shiny, smooth, satin, satin mat, mat, dry mat, and dry to indicate various states of glaze texture.

Surface quality is an important consideration in glazes, for it influences both the look of the glaze and its use. Ceramics intended for the table are usually glazed with shiny, smooth, or satin glazes; pieces that are not to be used with food may be finished with less easily cleaned glazes, such as those with mat or dry surfaces.

Glazes also have a visual texture. Many are completely smooth, especially in oxidation. Other glazes exhibit a rich variety of textures, including crystal patterns, light and dark modulations, pooling, and random flow.

Surface modulations are much valued because of their rich, varied, and often surprising qualities. Many have a way of emphasizing manipulations on the surface of the piece, an especially welcome characteristic. In the oxidation fire, these modulations combine the opportunity for rich surfaces associated with reduction with the brilliant high-key color associated with the oxidation fire.

Glaze Types

Another way potters distinguish among glazes is by characterizing the glaze according to its ingredients. This system is especially useful because strong similarities exist among glazes with similar ingredient combinations in terms of how they look and fire.

In the oxidation fire the following materials produce visual texture, especially in mat and satin mat glazes: wood ash, lithium compounds, bone ash (calcium phosphate), zirconium compounds, and barium carbonate.

Wood ash (the ash residue of wood fire) causes a modulated pattern of light and dark rivulets and small spots to occur on the surface of the glaze.

Lithium compounds cause a pattern of light and dark modulations on the glaze surface. These modulations are similar in pattern to salt glaze. Lithium also causes the glaze to pull away from the edges of the form. The result is a strange, halolike effect around the corners of the piece and around any manipulated imagery in the clay.

Bone ash encourages a soft spotted pattern to form in the glaze. Like lithium, it also encourages glaze to pull away from the edges of the form.

Zirconium compounds and *barium carbonate* cause a small crystal pattern to form on the surface of the glaze.

Depending on the nature of the cooling cycle, zinc oxide and titanium compounds cause crystal patterns to form within the glaze.

WOOD ASH GLAZES

Wood ash glazes are useful to the potter in oxidation. Rich, naturally textured, and somewhat unpredictable, when they are placed in an oxidation kiln the result is often beautiful.

3-7 Richard Zakin. Oswego, New York. Cone 6. This piece was finished by applying two different glazes, a smooth base glaze (G.K. white) and a textured glaze (Brutus Blue). A strong reaction between the two formulas caused a visual texture to form on the shoulder of the piece.

3-8 Richard Zakin. Oswego, New York. Cone 6. This textured glaze technique is effective on wheel-thrown work as well as hand-built pieces.

3-9 Richard Zakin. Oswego, New York. *Bottle*. Cone 6. Handbuilt, carved. Because the glazes used in this piece are translucent, they gather in the interstices and darken. This emphasizes the carved imagery.

3-10   Emmanuel Cooper. *Thrown Bowl.* 1260°C (approximately cone 8). Emmanuel Cooper works in oxidation-fired porcelain. He is able to produce richly colored and textured glazes for the electric kiln. This piece is a high clay mat glaze with a manganese-painted rim.

3-11   Emmanuel Cooper. *Thrown Bowl.* 1260°C (approximately cone 8). This is a zinc oxide glaze with some crystalline activity.

3-12　Emmanuel Cooper. London, England. 1260°C

3-13　Emmanuel Cooper. *Thrown Bowls*. 1260°C (approximately cone 8). Glazes high in nepheline syenite are used in these two bowls. Glazes of this sort can produce a rich crackle effect.

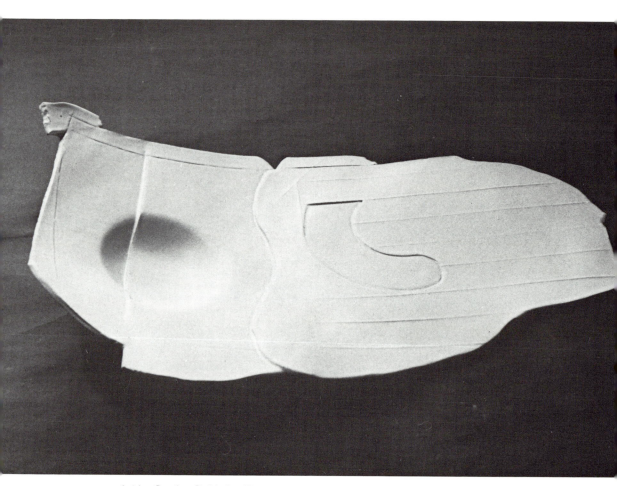

3-14 Gordon Baldwin. Eton,
Berkshire, England. *Platter Form*.
Cone 6. White fineclay covered with
an opaque white glaze. Baldwin has
used a simple, unassertive glaze
surface as a foil to the complicated
play of form and texture of this
piece.

3-15   Robert Forrest.
Rosendale, New York. Cone
9. Forrest has been working
intensively with crystal glazes.
He often applies these glazes
to bold thrown forms.

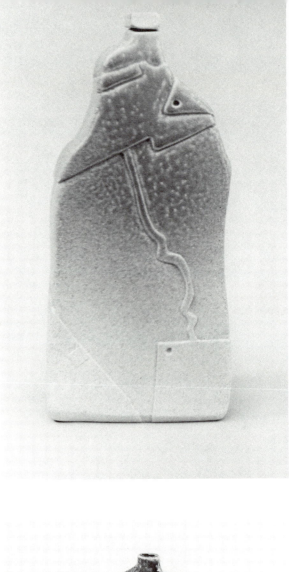

3-16 Richard Zakin. Oswego, New York. *Bottle*. Cone 6. Handbuilt, carved imagery, textured glazes. The carved imagery is a very important part of the total effect of this piece. I wanted a textured glaze effect that would enrich the surface without covering or blurring the carved imagery.

3-17 Richard Zakin. Oswego, New York. *Vase*. Cone 6. This piece is another example of a textured glaze surface used with carved imagery.

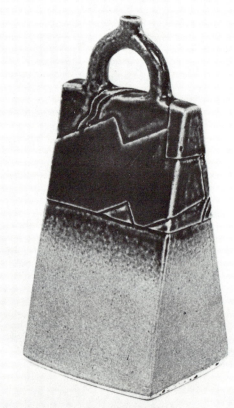

Wood ashes are complicated mixtures of coarse minerals, mostly fluxes, which melt unevenly in the glaze fire. They leave a tell-tale "calling card"; that is, the glaze melt has an uneven texture, marked by runny and comparatively refractory areas in close proximity. This results in the instantly recognized "wood ash texture."

Wood ash derives its character, including its flux content, from the tree the wood came from. Trees absorb minerals from the earth. These minerals vary from tree to tree, depending on the tree's environment and species. Wood ash therefore varies from batch to batch. Though many potters claim that certain fruitwoods give the best results, hardwood ash from a fireplace or wood stove is most satisfactory.

Wood ash from the Scandinavian air-tight stove is quite different from that of the old-fashioned fireplace; it contains a lower percentage of the fine-particled water-soluble fluxes that contribute so much to wood ash's strong texture. It still contributes texture, though somewhat less noticeably than fireplace wood ash. Comparatively clean and uniform, it needs little washing and screening.

It must be understood that wood ash is not a glaze but rather a glaze material. Because it is unpredictable, it is unwise to treat wood ash like other glaze materials, which are more uniform and consistent. Wood ash should be added to already complete glaze formulas. In this way it takes on the congenial role of a supplemental flux; wood ash can modify and enrich the glaze while deriving the benefits of stability and consistency from the basic glaze formula. I use wood ash as an additive to familiar glazes in amounts that vary from five to thirty percent of the total glaze weight. If the addition does not texture the glaze as much as I would like, I simply add more wood ash. If the glaze is unstable, running and flowing too much, I add more of the basic glaze formula.

SLIP GLAZES
Slip glazes are made totally or primarily from slip clay. Slip clays are high in fluxing and coloring impurities; they will form a glaze with little help from added fluxes if they are fired to stoneware temperatures. Slip glazes have been great favorites of Chinese and Japanese potters, whose work has been so influential on potters in our time. Many beautiful examples of this oriental slip-glazed work are found in museums and collections.

In the United States and Canada, potters have access to several excellent slip clays used for slip glazing. Two that are especially well known are Albany and Michigan slip clay. Many other fine slip clays can be used from local sources.

Slip clays contain such fluxing oxides as calcium, magnesium, manganese, iron, and titanium. These impurities usually make this material useless as an ingredient in a clay body, but they improve the clay's performance as a glaze material. High impurity clays are almost complete glazes in themselves; the addition of only a small amount of flux (about 10 percent) is enough to turn this material into a fine glaze at cones 5 to 10.

Slip glazes may be brown, green, or mustard and, with the addition of colorants, soft green, blue, burnt orange, and black.

Below are the analyses of Albany slip clay and, as a contrast, a kaolin,

3-18　Richard Zakin. Oswego, New York. *Platter*. Mouse Black in the interstices. A local slip glaze was splashed over part of the piece; it was then dipped in a clear wood ash glaze. The highly marked texture results from wood ash from a fireplace rather than from an airtight stove; wood ash from airtight stoves gives a less mottled texture.

3-19 Lynn Robinson. Toronto, Ontario. Cone 9. Robinson works with wood ash glazes fired in the electric kiln, achieving rich warm glaze surfaces. Although at first glance the overall effect may seem that of a reduction piece, these pieces have the brilliance and clarity associated with the oxidation fire.

3-20 Lynn Robinson. Toronto, Ontario. Cone 9. Wood ash fired in the electric kiln.

3-21 Wayne Cardinelli. Stirling, Ontario. Cone 6. Cardinelli says of his work:
"Oxidation was to be a brief interlude for me until I could build another salt kiln, at
which point I had planned to drop oxidation like a cold potato. That was about three
years ago, and the need for a new salt kiln is now rather low on my list of priorities. I
had a mistaken idea about the possibilities of oxidation but have found that I'm able
to attain glazes that are appropriate to the forms I make.

"I carried many of the decorating techniques I used with salt to my oxidation
glazing. I use four engobes, a few underglazes, an accent glaze, and usually an ash
glaze over the whole thing. This ash application works much like the salt did in
unifying the other engobe and glaze applications. The engobes burn through the
glazes, which are semitransparent. It is this multilayering (sometimes as many as
eight applications) that gives the glazes a visual depth.

"Rudi Staffel, my former teacher, once said that 'a pot is never more beautiful
than when it is freshly thrown, and the only reason to glaze is to make the pot look
wet again.' That is the quality I'm working for in my glazes; I want my fired pots to
look fluid again."

3-22 Jeanne McRight. Stirling,
Ontario. Cone 6.

3-23 Marc Barr. Memphis,
Tennesee. *Tea Set*. The insides of
these pieces were covered with a
slip glaze. On the outside a very
light coating of a wood ash glaze was
applied to the upper parts of the
pieces.

English china clay. Note the difference in the silica and alumina contents, as well as the difference in the amount and type of impurities.

	Albany Slip Clay	*English China Clay*
Silica	59.5	47.9
Alumina	11.5	37.3
Titanium	0.9	—
Fe_2O_3	4.1	0.5
Manganese	0.1	—
Calcium	6.3	—
Magnesium	3.4	0.1
Sodium	0.4	—
Potassium	2.8	1.9
Loss on Ignition (LOI)	11.0	12.3

Albany slip clay is much lower in alumina than is English china clay. Glazes made with a lot of Albany slip are therefore also low in alumina. The amount of alumina in a glaze profoundly affects its color, texture, and behavior in the fire.

The durable, varied and rich surfaces of many slip glazes derive their qualities from the high silica content of slip clays. Slip clays are complicated compounds. They may be used in the glaze as sources of silica, flux, and colorant; they are somewhat plastic and therefore help keep the glaze in suspension. Slip clays are valuable additions to any muted color glaze in proportions varying from 10 to 90 percent. In small amounts they serve to darken and flux the glaze; in large amounts they dominate the character of the glaze, muting its color and smoothing and hardening its surface.

Glazes made with more than 30 percent of slip clay often have some shrinkage. If they are applied to the bisque-fired piece, the glaze may shrink enough to flake and crack, or it may even fall off the piece and onto the kiln shelf. Therefore, when using glazes containing more than 30 percent slip clay, the potter should calcine some of the high flux clay. In the calcining process, the potter fires the dry slip clay in a bisque bowl to a temperature of 700°C. Calcined clay is, in a sense, preshrunk, which prevents glaze from shrinking and flaking on bisque. It is a good idea to leave 10–15 percent of the high flux clay uncalcined; the uncalcined clay, which is somewhat plastic, keeps the glaze in suspension.

TEXTURED GLAZES AND OVERGLAZES

Interesting results may be obtained with a family of glazes formulated from combinations of calcium, phosphorus, and lithium, often in a glaze containing a slip clay. Though these formulas fired at cones 3, 6, and 9 are not identical

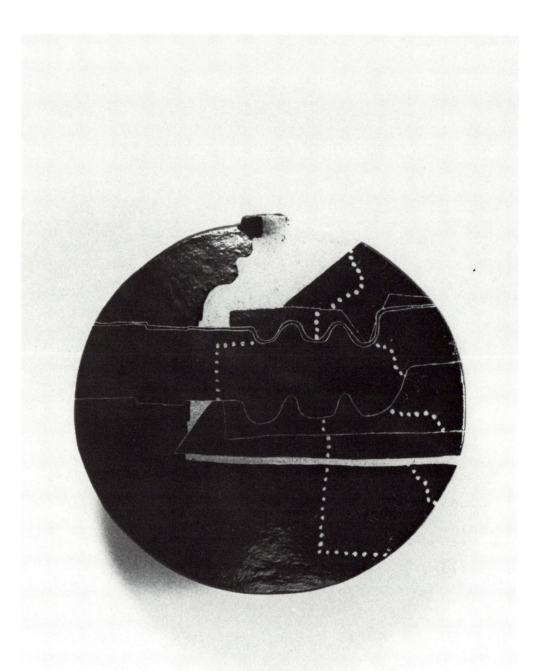

3-24   Richard Zakin. Oswego, New York. *Wall Hanging Vase*. Mouse Black slip glaze
applied to the leather-hard clay. The imagery was cut with a scratchboard tool.
During the fire the imagery neither blurred nor ran because a slip glaze was used.

90

3-25 This piece was ruined by glaze crawling. At the early stage of the firing, a good deal of the slip glaze cracked off the shoulder of the piece and fell onto the shelf. The glaze shrank away from the piece. The problem was solved in later firing by substituting calcined Albany slip clay for much of the slip clay in the formula.

in appearance, they all have a visual texture called "orange peel" (light and dark diverse patterning).

The texture of these glazes is shown best when they are applied by spraying. Some of these formulas are unstable, especially those intended for cones 3 and 6, and work best as overglazes. These are noted next to the formula.

4 *Glaze Color*

Since glazes are a sort of glass, it makes sense that they may be without color or opacity just as a window pane is without color or opacity. Most potters however, modify the clear glaze in some way. These modifications can be accomplished by adding some materials (called colorants) that color the glaze and other materials (called opacifiers) that make the glaze opaque. Colorants produce a wide range of color in the oxidation fire; opacified glazes give the potter opaque, white glazes. A glaze may contain both colorant and opacifier, and indeed a great many rich glaze formulations are based on this combination.

Glaze Colorants

Colorants are mineral compounds that have been chosen and prepared for the purpose of coloring ceramic glazes. They must be finely and uniformly ground, powerful and reliable. They are meant to be added to the glaze in varying amounts, usually 0.5 to 3 percent of the total formula. Not only do they directly influence the color of the glaze, but they in turn are influenced by the materials in the glaze.

Some of these materials are toxic, and care should be exercised in their use. There are simple procedures the potter can follow in using these invaluable materials safely and intelligently (see page 220).

The unfired color of the glaze colorants is not always the same as the color that the colorants impart to the glaze when it is fired. The color change that glazes undergo in the firing is one of the strange aspects of glazing. The potter becomes familiar with the color changes that take place in the firing and learns to deal with these changes at least most of the time, but even an experienced potter occasionally is surprised by what happens in the glaze kiln.

GLAZE COLORANTS IN OXIDATION

Colorant	0.5%	1%	2%	3%
iron oxide*	tan or cream	light orange or light yellow, gray-green	orange or yellow gray green	orange, brown, or gray green
cobalt oxide	pale blue	light blue	medium blue	very dark blue
cobalt carbonate	very pale blue	pale blue	light blue	medium to dark blue
copper oxide	pale green	light to medium green	medium to dark green	dark green to black
copper carbonate	very pale green	pale green	medium green	dark green to black
manganese oxide	pale plum or pink	light plum, pink or tan	plum or tan	deep plum or brown
rutile**	pale burnt orange	light burnt orange	medium burnt orange	dark burnt orange
chrome oxide	pale tan green	light tan green	tan green	heavy deep green

*This colorant is used in amounts up to 14 percent; it then tends to browns or reds.
**With equal amounts of iron.

Commercial Glaze Stains

One of the most persuasive reasons for working with oxidation glazes is the availability of a broad spectrum of commercial glaze stains. These colors are brilliant, safe to use, and very reliable. They are relatively expensive, but their usefulness and beauty are worth the price. Especially recommended are the yellows, oranges, and pinks.

These stains are introduced into stable white or clear glaze formulas in proportions ranging from 1 to 5 percent. They are most useful over white or porcelain-type bodies, or white slips.

Because they are fritted (that is, bonded with alumina, silica, and flux to make a glass), they are completely safe.

Glaze stains are made by commercial firms such as Hommel and Masons. They are intended for dinnerware and sanitary ware.

Glaze Problems

Oxidation potters fall heir to problems as often as reduction potters. Though shivering is not a big problem in oxidation, crawling is. Crawling may be caused by glazes that are over flocculated; that is, they are too sticky and shrink too much. In such a case, the potter may substitute calcined clay for some of the clay in the formula. Crawling also occurs when the glaze is too thick or if the pot is too wet (if you rinse the glaze off of a pot, let it dry for a few hours before trying to glaze it again) or dusty (blow the dust off the form). Sometimes crawling occurs when a wet glaze is applied over a dry one. If you are glazing in layers, let the first glaze set, but do not let it dry completely.

Some glazes, especially those containing bone ash and lithium, sink to the bottom of the bucket and harden there. Brutus base sinks like a stone to the bottom of the bucket, gathering in layers like some primeval sediment. If an object is glazed at this point, the fired result is poor, for many of the important glaze materials remain at the bottom of the bucket. There are two solutions to this problem. Either add a glaze flocculent, such as bentonite, vinegar, or yogurt (yogurt works very well, but it eventually causes a strange odor to form), or add precipitated magnesium carbonate, substituting it for another flux. This stops settling for good, although it sometimes radically alters the look of the glaze as well.

Vitreous Slips and Engobes

Vitreous means glasslike. Glazes are expected to be vitreous, but slips and engobes, with their high clay content, usually are not; nevertheless, some are. Their vitreous quality is a result of the presence of very strong fluxes in the formulation; these flux combinations are powerful enough to vitrify high clay formulations. Such formulas tend to be stable and durable.

Vitreous engobes are high clay formulas (25 to 50 percent clay) whose flux content is powerful enough to insure that a glassy melt results in the firing. They may be used in concert with stains and glazes as a sort of foundation glaze or underglaze, or they may be used alone. If vitreous engobes are used as foundation glazes, they are stable and compatible with other materials. If vitreous engobes are used alone, they are shiny and look and feel like glazes. They are high in alumina, which contributes viscosity, and will not run or blur in the fire. It is thus possible to develop a technique that combines the richness and durability of glazes with the graphic, painterly qualities of engobes.

It is important to remember that many of these high clay slips and engobes shrink a great deal. If they are applied to bisque-fired ware, much of their clay content should be calcined.

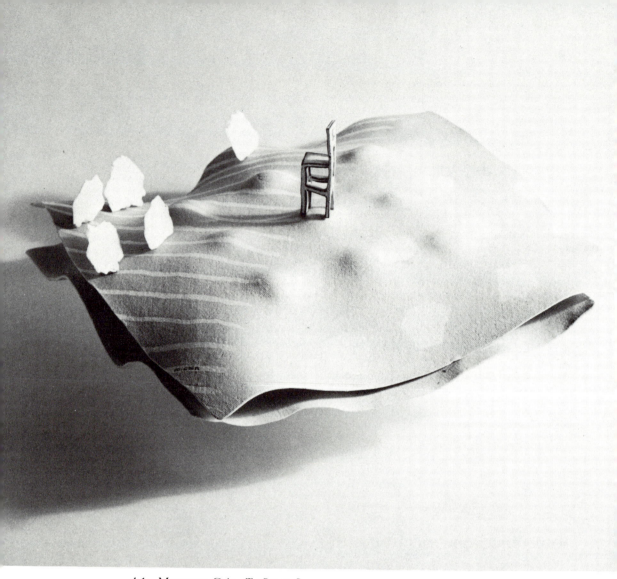

4-1 Maryanne Cain. *To Sea to See.*
Cone 6. Handbuilt, assembled after
firing. Cain used glaze stains to
produce results that in brilliance
rival the low fire. She attains the
strength of high fire clay and glazes
and the exciting tonalities of the low
fire.

4-2 Richard Zakin. Oswego, New York. *Plaque.* Cone 6. Handbuilt. This piece is glazed with a vitreous engobe. Although the surface is very soft and waxy looking, it is quite strong and durable. Unlike normal slips or engobes, vitreous engobes are often translucent. Underglaze effects, such as black glaze in the interstices, bleed through the engobe much as they would through a glaze.

4-3 Richard Zakin. Oswego, New York. *Bowl.* Cone 6. Handbuilt. This piece was formed with a dark clay body (August I) that encourages rich but somber glaze color. An opaque vitreous engobe (August Engobe) was splashed over part of the piece. The result is that the glaze varies in color, depending on whether it is over the dark clay or the light engobe.

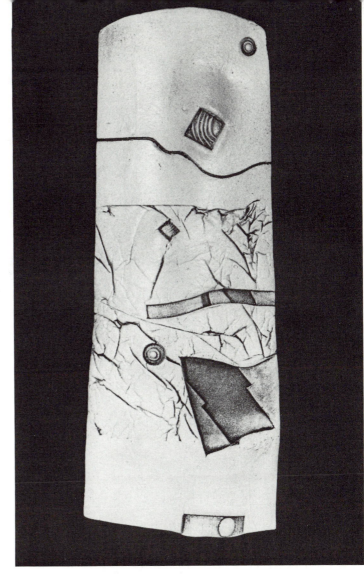

4-4 Elizabeth Fritsch. London,
England. *Vases*. Cone 8. Handbuilt.
Fritsch uses a vitreous engobe of her
own devising. This formula has a
rich, waxy, mat finish; if used with
painted imagery, it does not blur or
distort in the fire. The combination
of these two characteristics is
difficult to obtain. The result is a
graphic imagery of great richness
and detail. Fritsch handles her
materials with freedom and
virtuosity.

4-5 Elizabeth Fritsch. London,
England.

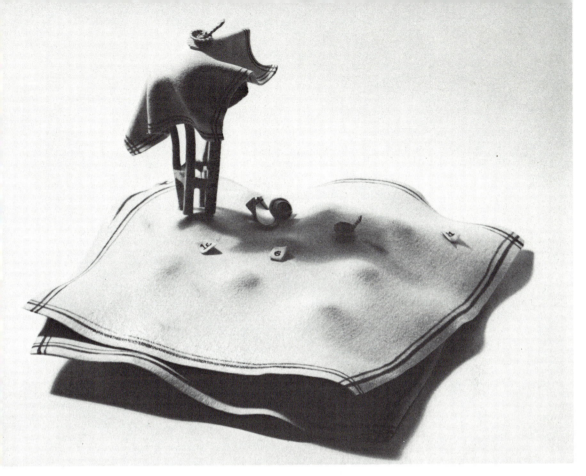

4-6 Maryanne Cain. Toronto, Ontario. *For Tea # 2*. Cone 6.

4-7 Maryanne Cain. Toronto, Ontario. *Right Of Way*. Cone 6.

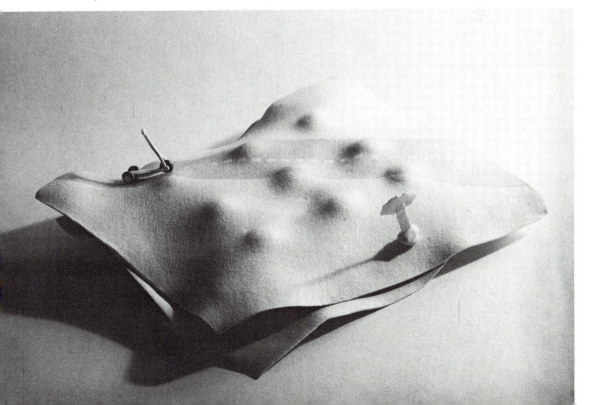

Cone 3 Glazes

Cone 3 offers a wide choice of color and rich, visually textured glaze effects.

The glaze experimenter has somewhat less leeway at cone 3 than at higher temperature ranges. This is because cone 3 glazes require fairly strong flux combinations, and some of these combinations do not encourage glaze stability. Stable mat-surfaced glazes are especially difficult to achieve.

Cone 3 leadless glazes must be very strongly fluxed to be useful at this comparatively low temperature. Since these strong flux combinations can affect stability adversely, it is difficult to develop formulas that are stable under all conditions. Great care should be taken in glazing, firing, and cooling. Slow cooling is particularly important. It is best to leave the kiln on a low (or very low) setting for a few hours after the ware has reached maturity, so that the glazes will have a chance to cool slowly and evenly.

The following formulas seem to offer the best combination of interesting color characteristics and usefulness.

TRANSPARENT GLAZE

Index Transparent Glaze

Soda spar	46%	*This is a hard-surfaced, durable,*
Flint	18	*transparent glaze. It is excellent for table*
Gerstley borate	18	*use, as knives neither mark it nor make*
Ball clay	6	*an unpleasant sound in contact with it.*
Wollastonite	6	
Barium carbonate	2	
Zinc	2	
Lithium carbonate	2	

TRANSLUCENT GLAZE

Maplegrove Translucent Base

Nepheline syenite	40%	*This is a clear, rich, durable glaze.*
Wollastonite	16	
Flint	14	
Kaolin	12	
Gerstley borate	8	
Bone ash	4	
Zinc	4	
Lithium carbonate	2	
Copper carbonate	2	
—a soft, clear green		
Cobalt oxide	1	
Rutile	4	
—a clear, medium blue		

Elk Creek Translucent Glaze

Soda feldspar	32%	*This is a soft, grassy green. Its surface is*
Gerstley borate	20	*fairly mat.*
Albany slip clay	16	
Talc	14	
Barium	12	
Flint	6	
Copper carbonate	2	

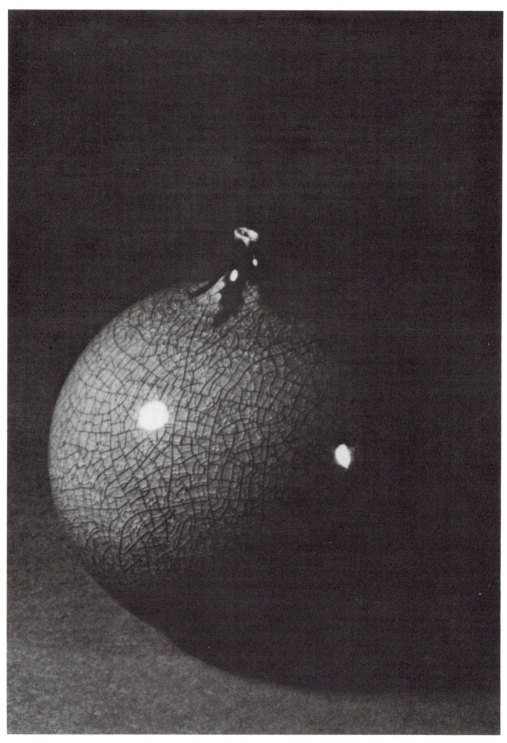

4-8   Karl Martz. Bloomington, Indiana. Cone 3.

Carmel Glaze

Albany slip clay	60%	*A soft looking, pale amber glaze; where*
Gerstley borate	20	*thin it becomes a burnt orange.*
Ball clay	10	
Dolomite	10	

Treadwell Base

Albany slip clay	88%	*A very dark brown glaze. Strong and du-*
Gerstley borate	10	*rable. Treadwell is an excellent "liner*
Lithium carbonate	1.7	*glaze." Use the base formula with 8 per-*
Zinc	0.3	*cent iron oxide and 2 percent manganese*
		dioxide to obtain a rich brown glaze.
Cobalt oxide	2	

Milford Burnt Orange

Albany slip clay	79.5%	*This a rich, deep, burnt orange glaze. It*
Gerstley borate	7	*works very well with the Fabius texture*
Talc	6	*glazes.*
Ball clay	5	
Lithium carbonate	2	
Zinc	0.5	

OPAQUE GLAZES

The two glaze formulas that follow contain zirconium opacifier and are somewhat opaque.

Richmondville Glaze

Soda feldspar	30%	*This is a very durable, hard-surfaced*
Albany slip clay	20	*glaze, pale straw yellow in color.*
Ball clay	20	
Gerstley borate	16	
Dolomite	8	
Zircopax	6	

Snyders Glaze

Albany slip clay	30%	*A soft-looking, earth yellow. Where very*
Soda spar	26	*thin it is amber-orange.*
Gerstley borate	14	
Dolomite	12	
Ball clay	10	
Zircopax	8	

TEXTURED GLAZES

Neither of the two glaze formulas that follow are meant to function as a base glaze; rather, they are to be used over other glazes. When used in this way they react with the base glaze, resulting in a rich texture. This texture expresses itself in an "orange peel" pattern of light and dark modulation. Although this kind of texture is associated with salt firing—and, to a lesser extent, with wood ash glazes—these formulas give this effect as well. The essential ingredients in these glazes are lithium and phosphorus (in the bone ash), which react with calcium (in the dolomite) and iron oxide (in the Albany slip clay).

Texture glazes are best applied by spraying, which encourages the "orange peel" texture to form. If you do not have a spray outfit, a small, inexpensive sprayer-atomizer is suitable. This is an excellent tool for applying glaze in a localized area.

These glazes have a light orange cast from the Albany slip clay content. They will darken and color any glazes they are applied over.

Fabius Texture Glaze I

Albany slip clay	40%
Dolomite	26
Gerstley borate	24
Lithium carbonate	4
Bone ash	4
Barium carbonate	2

Albany slip clay	40%
Dolomite	28
Gerstley borate	20
Lithium carbonate	4
Bone ash	4
Frit 3124 (or Frit 90)	4

The Fabius II formula tends to be more stable than Fabius I; its texture, however, is less rich.

4-9   Richard Zakin. Oswego,
New York. Cone 3. A group
of pieces from a cone 3 test
firing.

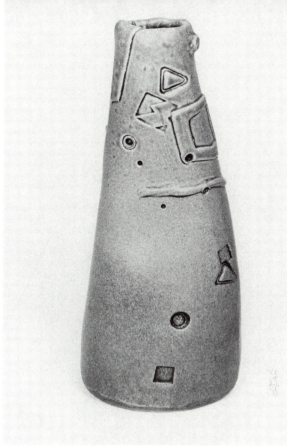

4-10 Richard Zakin.
Oswego, New York. Cone 3.
This piece was glazed in the
following manner: Treadwell
Base with iron and manganese
daubed in the interstices,
Milford glaze over all, Fabius
I at the top.

4-11 Richard Zakin.
Oswego, New York. Cone 3.
This piece is glazed with
Maplegrove Green and Fabius
I with 2 percent cobalt.

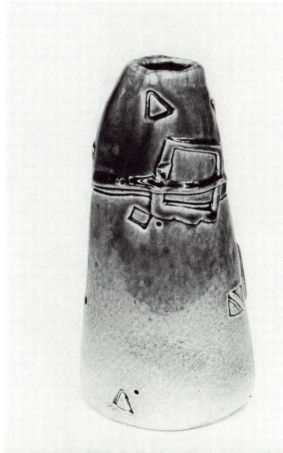

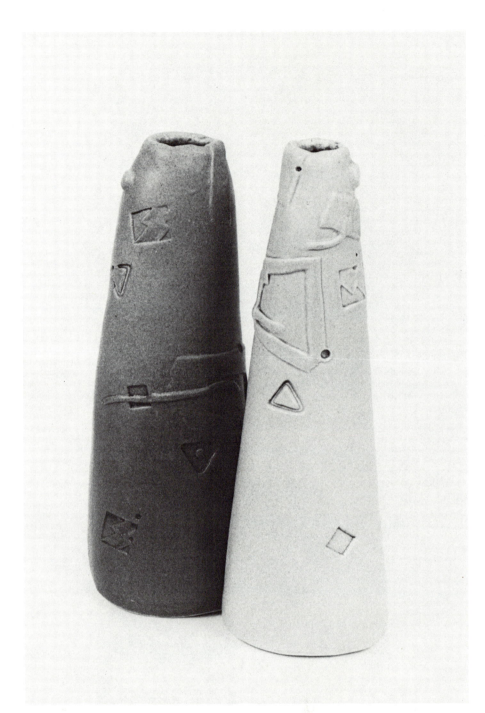

4-12 Richard Zakin. Oswego, New York. Cone 3. Both of these pieces were
prepared for glazing by the application of Treadwell Base, with iron and manganese,
in the interstices. The vase on the left was glazed with the Milford glaze overall and
the Fabius II texture glaze sprayed at the top. The piece on the right was glazed
with the Snyder's glaze overall and the Fabius II texture glaze sprayed at the top.

Cone 6 Glazes

Cone 6 glazes offer the advantages of durability, stability, and richness. A wide range of formulas can be used with confidence. Even at this comparatively high temperature, a diversity of color and tone is available.

TRANSPARENT GLAZES

Volcanic Ash Clear (low crackle)

Volcanic ash	40%	*No colorant—a hard, very clear,*
Gerstley borate	12	*transparent glaze.*
Barium carbonate	6	
Wollastonite	10	
Flint	18	
Ball clay	12	
Zinc oxide	2	

Soft Waxy Transparent

Nepheline syenite	45%	*No colorant—a transparent glaze with a*
Barium	8	*slight iron coloration. This glaze has some*
Gerstley borate	22	*crackle effect.*
Wollastonite	14	
Ball clay	8	
Zinc oxide	3	

Tyler Amber

Albany slip clay	80%	*No colorant—a rich brown amber.*
Gerstley borate	10	
Nepheline syenite	10	

Transparent Wood Ash Glaze

Unwashed wood ash (dry)	50%	*Proportions by volume. This may need adjustment.*
Transparent glaze	50	

TRANSLUCENT GLAZES

Lombard Base

Albany slip clay	25%
Gerstley borate	20
Ball clay	22
Nepheline syenite	14
Spodumene	12
Magnesium carbonate	7
Copper carbonate	2

—brown-green, translucent, celadonlike

Iron	2
Rutile	2

—a rich brown, pools well

Wollastonite V Base

Albany slip clay	5%	*No colorant—soft yellow ochre, some visual texture.*
Wollastonite	35	
Ball clay	40	
Nepheline syenite	15	
Gerstley borate	5	

Phoenix Base

Barnard slip clay	20%	*If applied thickly, this glaze may run.*
Ball clay	20	
Wollastonite	30	
Gerstley borate	30	
Rutile	1	
—*burnt orange*		

Corinth Base Glaze

Wollastonite	15%	*No colorant—light straw color.*
Barium	25	
Flint	5	
Albany slip clay	15	
Nepheline syenite	25	
Soda feldspar	15	
Copper carbonate	3	
—*strong green with a slight bluish cast*		
Cobalt oxide	2	
—*royal blue*		

Karen's Glaze

Nepheline syenite	40%	*A rich green; developed by Karen*
Dolomite	20	*Lindenberger in a class under my*
Flint	20	*direction.*
Kaolin	10	
Bone ash	6	
Zinc oxide	4	
Copper carbonate	2	

K. 15 I

Nepheline syenite	40%	*This glaze is very rich in color and*
Dolomite	18	*surface. It may be used by itself or in*
Flint	18	*concert with other glazes. It is especially*
Kaolin	12	*effective with the Brutus glaze, and with*
Bone ash	6	*the Burlington vitreous engobe.*
Lithium carbonate	2	
Zinc oxide	4	
Copper carbonate	2	

K. 15 II

Nepheline syenite	40%	*This glaze is similar to K. 15 I, but its*
Wollastonite	18	*higher silica content (from the*
Flint	18	*Wollastonite) makes it more translucent.*
Kaolin	12	
Bone ash	6	
Zinc oxide	4	
Lithium carbonate	2	
Copper carbonate	2	

K. 15 III

Nepheline syenite	42%	*This glaze also is a variation of K. 15 I,*
Flint	20	*but is perhaps somewhat smoother with*
Dolomite	14	*less visual texture.*
Kaolin	12	
Bone ash	6	
Zinc oxide	4	
Lithium carbonate	2	
Copper carbonate	2	

Gower Base

Nepheline syenite	33%	A *shiny, translucent glaze, very smooth,*
Barium carbonate	24	*hard, and abrasion resistant.*
Flint	23	
Gerstley borate	10	
Ball clay	6	
Whiting	3	
Magnesium carbonate	1	
Copper carbonate	1.5	

Chenies Base

Soda feldspar	31%	A *satin-mat, translucent glaze base.*
Spodumene	15	
Barium carbonate	15	
Zirconium opacifier	12	
Gerstley borate	8	
Magnesium carbonate	7	
Whiting	6	
Kaolin	6	
Copper carbonate	1.5	

4-13 Pat Doran. Boston,
Massachusetts. Cone 6. These
pieces were glazed in the following
manner: K.15 with 3 percent rutile
was applied over the whole piece by
dipping. The same base, with an
addition of chrome, cobalt, and
rutile, was then sprayed over the
shoulders and tops of the forms.
The clay body is a cone 6 porcelain
type.

4-14 Richard Zakin. Oswego, New York. Cone 6. This piece was glazed with K 15 overall. Brutus Blue was applied in selected areas.

OPAQUE GLAZES

T.Z. Dry Base Glaze

Ball clay	26%	*No colorant—a fine, dry white.*
Wollastonite	28	
Nepheline syenite	35	
Tin oxide	8	
Zinc oxide	3	

Troy II Base

Barium	10%	*No colorant—pure white.*
Gerstley borate	16	
Nepheline syenite	28	
Opax	11	
Wollastonite	20	
Six Tile kaolin	10	
Flint	5	
Cobalt	1.5	
—*rich medium blue*		
Copper carbonate	2	
—*strong green*		
Iron	1.5	
Rutile	1.5	
—*rich burnt orange*		

Zinc Glaze

Zinc oxide	22%	*No colorant—a bright white.*
Whiting	17	
Ball clay	17	
Flint	11	
Nepheline syenite	33	

Mississippi Copper Blue Green

Flint	15%
Ball clay	15
Soda feldspar	20
Dolomite	20
Gerstley borate	12
Wollastonite	10
Opax	8
Copper carbonate	1.2
—*brilliant copper blue*	

This rich, smooth-surfaced glaze was developed by Joan Mathieu in a class under my direction.

Coburg Base

Potash feldspar	41%
Whiting	15
Barium carbonate	14
Kaolin	13
Zirconium opacifier	9
Gerstley borate	8

A satin-mat, opaque glaze base.

Variation Base

Nepheline syenite	35%
Barium carbonate	20
Gerstley borate	13
Dolomite	12
Zircopax	10
Kaolin	5
Flint	5
Cobalt	1.5
—*mid blue*	
Copper carbonate	2
—*turquoise green*	

No colorant—mat white.

G.K.

Frit 90 or 3124	18%	*No colorant—over stoneware, a soft broken white; over porcelain, a smooth, hard, ivory white. This glaze has a strong visual texture.*
Magnesium carbonate	7	
Nepheline syenite	10	
Barium carbonate	15	
Spodumene	15	
Kaolin	10	
White	13	
Opax	12	
Copper	2	
—*copper blue*		

Zakin Base

Nepheline syenite	35%	*No colorant—mat white.*
Gerstley borate	20	
Barium carbonate	12	
Zircopax	10	
Flint	8	
Magnesium carbonate	5	
Whiting	5	
Ball clay	5	
Cobalt	1.5	
—*mid blue with violet overtones*		
Iron	2	
Rutile	1	
—*very rich burnt orange*		
Copper oxide	2	
—*rich green*		

Yrex Base

Albany slip clay	40%	*No colorant—very soft mat orange to tan.*
Ball clay	20	
Whiting	30	
Bone ash	10	

Troy Base

Nepheline syenite	30%	*No colorant—mat white.*
Wollastonite	20	
Gerstley borate	20	
Ball clay	10	
Barium carbonate	10	
Zircopax	10	
Cobalt *—mid blue*	1.5	
Iron	2	
Rutile *—burnt orange*	1	
Copper carbonate *—turquoise green*	2	

Gumrak Base

Frit 3124 or 90	23%	*No colorant—mat white. This glaze has a*
Potash spar	5	*strong visual texture.*
Nepheline syenite	10	
Barium carbonate	15	
Spodumene	15	
Kaolin	10	
Whiting	13	
Zircopax	9	
Iron	2	
Rutile	2	
—extremely rich burnt orange		

Cardington Base

Nepheline syenite	37%	*No colorant—tan orange. This glaze has a strong visual texture.*
Barium carbonate	24	
Flint	15	
Gerstley borate	14	
Ball clay	5	
Dolomite	5	
Cobalt —*gray blue*	1	
Iron oxide	3	
Rutile —*a burnt orange*	1	

Drummond Base

Wollastonite	30%	*A satin glaze.*
Soda feldspar	22	
Spodumene	12	
Kaolin	10	
Barium carbonate	10	
Opax	8	
Flint	6	
Bone ash	2	

Troy IV Base

Nepheline syenite	30%	*A strongly textured translucent formula. Like Cardington, it is very durable.*
Wollastonite	20	
Ball clay	20	
Gerstley borate	10	
Barium carbonate	10	
Zirconium opacifier	10	

Waterford Base

Nepheline syenite	30%	*This is a smooth satin mat with some visual texture.*
Wollastonite	20	
Gerstley borate	18	
Ball clay	10	
Barium carbonate	10	
Opax	9	
Lithium carbonate	2.5	
Zinc oxide	0.5	

Satin Mat I

Barium carbonate	10%	*A soft opaque mat.*
Gerstley borate	20	
Nepheline syenite	30	
Wollastonite	20	
Zirconium silicate opacifier	10	
Ball clay	10	

Satin Mat II

Barium carbonate	10%	*An opaque satin glaze.*
Gerstley borate	16	
Nepheline syenite	28	
Wollastonite	11	
Zirconium silicate opacifier	20	
Kaolin	10	
Silica	5	

TEXTURED GLAZES

The Brutus textured glazes, like their cone 3 textured glaze counterparts, are not meant to be used as base glazes but rather over a base glaze to add texture and interest. These glazes are very active and react with most other glazes in an "orange peel" texture. To get the maximum "orange peel" effect, it is best to spray textured glazes. If you do not have a spray outfit, use an atomizer-sprayer to apply these glazes in a localized area.

Brutus Base

Albany slip clay	43%	*No colorant—tan-orange. This glaze has a*
Wollastonite	38	*strong visual texture.*
Whiting	15	
Lithium	2	
Bone ash	2	
Cobalt	1	
—*gray-blue*		
Iron	3	
Rutile	1	
—*orange*		

Brutus II S.R.P.

Albany slip clay	42%
Wollastonite	38
Dolomite	14
Lithium carbonate	2
Bone ash	2
Zinc oxide	2

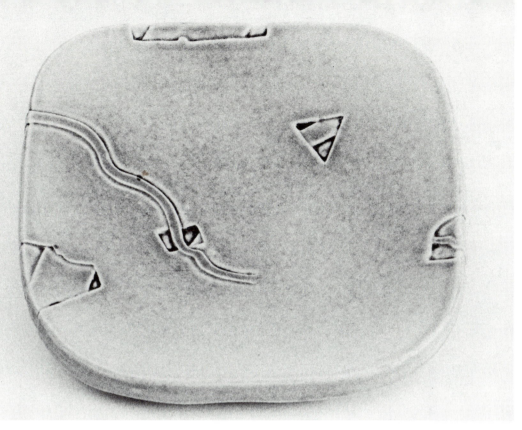

4-15   Richard Zakin. Oswego, New York. Cone 6. This piece was glazed simply. Mouse Black glaze was daubed in the interstices and cleaned, then K 15 glaze was sprayed over the whole piece.

4-16   Richard Zakin. Oswego, New York. Cone 6. This piece was glazed with K 15 overall. The lip and shoulder were sprayed with Burlington with 2 percent cobalt oxide.

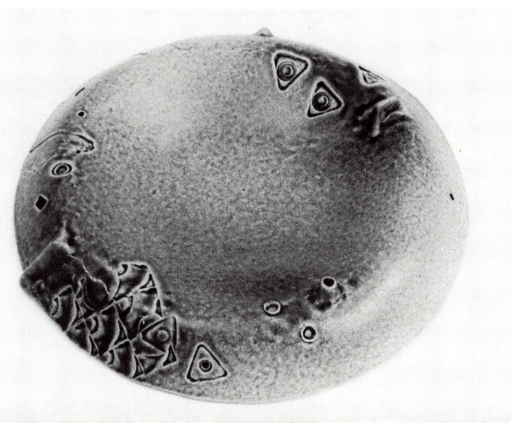

SLIP GLAZES

Mouse Black

Albany slip clay	85%
Nepheline syenite	5
Wollastonite	10
Cobalt oxide	2

A rich black glaze, especially useful as a "liner" for the inside of a vessel.

Dry Black

Albany slip clay	65%
Ball clay	25
Wollastonite	5
Borax	5
Cobalt oxide	2

Rich and black, this is more mat than Mouse Black; it is also quite durable.

Wollastonite II Base

Albany slip clay	40%
Ball clay	25
Wollastonite	20
Nepheline syenite	15
Cobalt	1.5

—a rich, muted blue

No colorant—a deep tan.

Wollastonite III Base

Albany slip clay	25%	*No colorant—light tan.*
Wollastonite	25	
Ball clay	30	
Nepheline syenite	15	
Gerstley borate	5	
Cobalt oxide *—rich, soft blue*	1.5	
Cobalt oxide	1.5	
Rutile *—soft iron blue*	1	
Copper carbonate *—soft, muted green*	2	

Wollastonite IV Base

Albany slip clay	25%	*No colorant—a muted tan with some*
Ball clay	30	*visual texture.*
Wollastonite	40	
Gerstley borate	5	

Pharsalia Base

Nepheline syenite	28%	*This glaze has a strong visual texture. It*
Albany slip clay	26	*is also quite durable.*
Dolomite	18	
Flint	12	
Kaolin	8	
Bone ash	4	
Lithium carbonate	2	
Zinc oxide	2	

Wollastonite 1 za

Albany slip clay	88%	*A rich umber black.*
Wollastonite	8.4	
Lithium carbonate	2	
Borax	1	
Zinc oxide	0.6	
Rutile	2	
Cobalt oxide	1.5	

VITREOUS ENGOBES

August Vitreous Engobe

E.P.K. kaolin	30%	*This is a very flat, smooth, durable sur-*
Frit 90 or 3124	20	*face, useful as an underglaze. It also may*
Flint	20	*be used alone. Its completely smooth sur-*
Nepheline syenite	20	*face contrasts nicely with visually textured*
Talc	10	*glazes.*

Semi Vit II

Frit 90 or 3124	45%	*An opaque vitreous engobe.*
E.P.K. kaolin	30	
Zircopax	12	
Flint	8	
Barium carbonate	5	

Semi Vit III

Frit 90 or 3124	48%	*Similar to the August Vitreous Engobe,*
E.P.K. kaolin	35	*but completely opaque.*
Zircopax	12	
Barium carbonate	5	

Burlington Base

Ball clay	25%
Albany slip clay	22
Soda spar	20
Zircopax	12
Whiting	12
Barium carbonate	7
Lithium carbonate	2
Copper carbonate 　*—a soft yellow-green*	2
Cobalt oxide 　*—a slate blue*	1
Manganese dioxide 　*—a brown-pink*	2

The Burlington Base has a rich inviting surface. It is also quite durable and can be used on tableware.

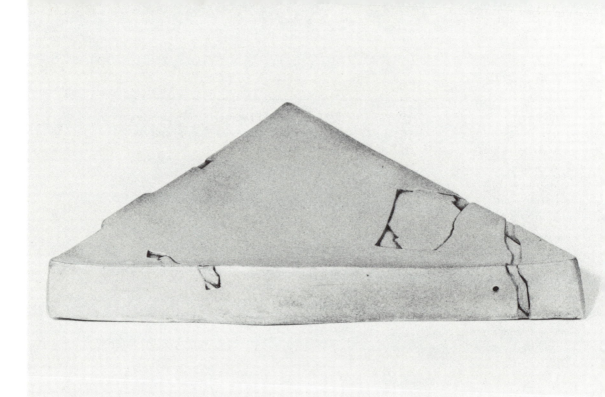

4-17 Richard Zakin. Oswego, New York. Cone 6. A table sculpture finished with Burlington vitreous engobe.

4-18 Richard Zakin. Oswego, New York. Cone 6. After glazing overall in Burlington with iron and cobalt, this piece was then sprayed with Brutus Blue.

Cone 9 Glazes

Cone 9 glazes tend to be very durable. The stable, high-fire fluxes calcium and magnesium are used frequently at this temperature. These glazes look subdued, earthy, and reserved, with very rich surfaces.

TRANSPARENT GLAZES

Northfield Transparent Glaze

Potash feldspar	35%	*A durable, clear glaze, useful and func-*
Flint	18	*tional. A knife will neither mark nor*
Wollastonite	15	*scratch it.*
Kaolin	14	
Barium	10	
Gerstley borate	6	
Zinc	2	

Andes Chun

Soda feldspar	40%	*This is a transparent, durable, rich, cop-*
Flint	27	*per green. It is quite shiny.*
Dolomite	16.7	
Barium	8	
Kaolin	4	
Lithium	2	
Tin oxide	2	
Zinc oxide	0.3	
Copper carbonate	2.5	

TRANSLUCENT GLAZES

Allen Creek Base

Potash feldspar	50%	*A translucent semimat with a soft surface.*
Ball clay	10	*This glaze was formulated by Lisa Booth*
Barium carbonate	15	*in a class under my direction.*
Talc	10	
Whiting	10	
Gerstley borate	5	

Troy Variation Base

Potash feldspar	30%	*A very strong surface, translucent and*
Gerstley borate	18	*fairly shiny.*
Flint	12	
Wollastonite	10	
Barium carbonate	10	
Ball clay	10	
Opax	10	

Trine Base

Potash feldspar	30%	*A soft-looking, milky, translucent glaze. A*
Wollastonite	20	*fairly shiny surface, abrasion resistant.*
Gerstley borate	16	
Ball clay	12	
Zircopax	12	
Barium carbonate	10	

Webster Base

Soda spar	30%	*This glaze was formulated by Lisa Booth*
Talc	20	*in a class under my direction.*
Wollastonite	15	
Flint	10	
Nepheline syenite	10	
Spodumene	10	
Ball clay	5	

Woodbourne Base

Albany slip clay	30%	*This glaze is a soft cream; its surface is a*
Dolomite	28	*smooth mat.*
Potspar	24	
Barium	10	
Ball clay	8	

4-19 Richard Zakin. Oswego, New
York. *Hanging Vase*. Cone 9.
Handbuilt, porcelain. A clear glaze
was applied to a white porcelain
body.

OPAQUE GLAZES

Cohoes Base

Potash feldspar	30%
Wollastonite	20
Gerstley borate	14
Kaolin	10
Barium	10
Opax	11
Flint	5

H.G.K. Base

Frit 90 or 3124	21%
Magnesium carbonate	7
Potash feldspar	10
Barium	15
Spodumene	15
Kaolin	10
Whiting	10
Opax	12

G.K.N. Base

Barium carbonate	17%
Spodumene	17
Whiting	16
Magnesium carbonate	14
Opax	14
Frit 90 or 3124	11
Kaolin	11

This is a soft-looking, mat white with a fairly strong visual texture. It has a rich, inviting surface.

Lamson Base

Soda spar	40%	
Barium carbonate	35	
Albany slip clay	12	
Flint	8	
Spodumene	5	
Copper carbonate	2	

A soft, opaque glaze. There is some crazing where it is thick. A soft blue-green in color.

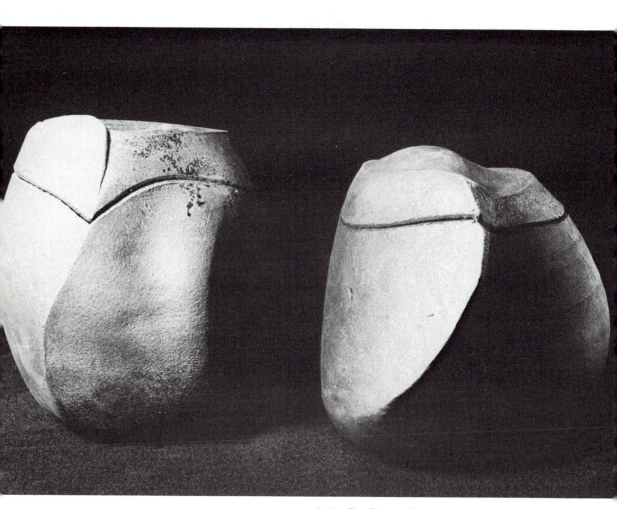

4-20 Pat Doran. Boston, Massachusetts. Cone 9. These pieces were glazed with a high-mat white formula over a porcelain body.

Godffroy Green

Wollastonite	25%	*A soft green with a very slight texture.*
Kaolin	24	
Potash feldspar	17	
Gerstley borate	12	
Barium	11	
Opax	9	
Zinc oxide	2	
Copper carbonate	2	

Lewbeach

Potash feldspar	30%	*A very rich, saturated, copper green glaze. The glaze seems to pull away from ridges and corners handsomely.*
Dolomite	16	
Opax	12	
Gerstley borate	10	
Kaolin	10	
Barium	8	
Bone ash	8	
Lithium carbonate	4	
Zinc oxide	2	
Copper carbonate	2	

Hamden Green

Potash feldspar	30%	*A soft-looking mat glaze, green where thick and white where thin.*
Dolomite	18	
Opax	12	
Gerstley borate	10	
Kaolin	10	
Barium carbonate	10	
Lithium carbonate	4	
Bone ash	4	
Zinc oxide	2	
Copper carbonate	2	

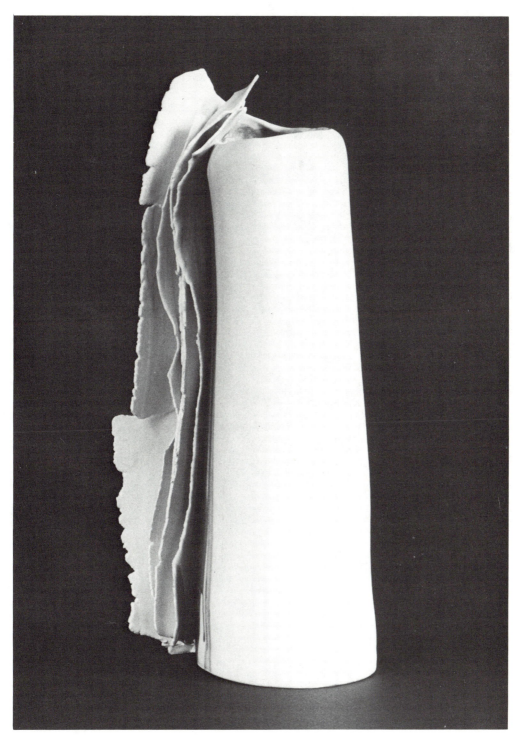

4-21 Marylyn Dintenfass. Mamaroneck, New York. *Vase.* Cone 9. Handbuilt. This piece is covered with a milky white, fairly opaque glaze.

4-22 Val Barry. London, England.
Vases. Cone 9. Handbuilt. These
pieces have a beautiful opaque mat
surface. *Photo by Ian Yeomans*

4-23 Phyllis Ihrman. Detroit,
Michigan. *Vase Group*. Cone 9/10.
Ihrman has developed a whole
group of methods for dealing with
the problems of the oxidation fire,
porcelain, single firing, and low-
alumina glazes (both flowing mats
and crystal glazes). In these pieces
she has used a low-alumina, high-
alkaline mat glaze type.

4-24 Phyllis Ihrman. Detroit, Michigan. *Carved Vase.* Cone 9/10.

4-25 Paul Astbury. London, England. Cone 9/10. Astbury attains in the oxidation fire a rich, mysterious glaze surface that complements the stark drama of his imagery.

4-26 Eileen Lewenstein. Sussex,
England. *Covered Jars*. Cone 9.
Many materials used for producing
visual texture in cone 6 oxidation
glazes can be used for the same
purpose at cone 9. These include
materials containing lithium,
zirconium, phosphorus, and fluorine.
The effect is quite rich.

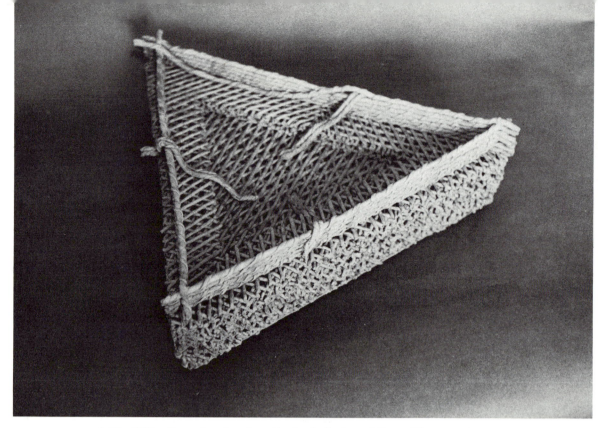

4-27 Gillian Lowndes. London, England. *Sculptural Form*. The complicated form is finished in a simple, stony surface—a mat glaze most probably high in aluminum and calcium.

4-28 Gillian Lowndes. London, England. *Sculptural Form*. This piece is finished with a stony mat surface.

ALBANY SLIP CLAY GLAZES

Gateville Base

Albany slip clay	70%	*This glaze was formulated by Laura*
Magnesium carbonate	10	*Molascon in a class under my direction. It*
Potash feldspar	10	*is a rich, shiny brown with some breakup*
Bone ash	10	*and good abrasion resistance.*

Brutus Variation Base

Albany slip clay	40%	*This glaze is liberally marked with visual*
Wollastonite	40	*texture. It has a very rich, vivid texture.*
Whiting	16	*Without colorants, it is tan in color.*
Lithium carbonate	2	
Bone ash	2	

Conquest Base

Albany slip clay	80%	*A rich, deep, shiny brown. It seems to*
Potash feldspar	10	*combine well with other glazes.*
Bone ash	10	

Lysander Base

Albany slip clay	25%	*Tan where thin, gray-black where thick.*
Ball clay	22	*Some visual texture, a rich surface.*
Wollastonite	20	
Potash feldspar	14	
Spodumene	12	
Magnesium carbonate	7	
Copper carbonate	2	

Parkside Variation Base

Albany slip clay	37%	*A soft translucent tan where thin, brown-*
Whiting	18	*pink where thick. Mat surface.*
Spodumene	15	
Flint	10	
Ball clay	10	
Zinc oxide	5	
Bone ash	5	

Volney Base

Albany slip clay	80%	*A soft-looking brown glaze, brown-red*
Wollastonite	10	*where thin and deep brown where thick.*
Potash feldspar	10	

Macc. Base

Albany slip clay	25%	*A rich-textured, mat glaze formula.*
Ball clay	40	
Magnesium carbonate	28	
Bone ash	3	
Spodumene	4	

TEXTURED GLAZES

Crucial in these textured glazes is calcium, which works well at cone 9. Many of these glazes also include Cedar Heights Redart, which is midway between kaolin and Albany slip clay.

Unlike the cone 3 and cone 6 textured glazes, these cone 9 glazes can be used alone as well as in concert with other glazes.

Kortright Textured Glaze

Cedar Heights Redart	32%	
Dolomite	28	
Ball clay	24	
Barium carbonate	8	
Bone ash	6	
Lithium carbonate	2	

Where thick, this glaze is translucent yellow; where thin, it reveals the color of the clay body. Its appearance is similar to wood ash glaze.

Shandaken Textured Glaze

Cedar Heights Redart	40%	
Dolomite	32	
Ball clay	20	
Bone ash	6	
Lithium carbonate	2	

A rich, burnt orange glaze. The texture expresses itself in an overall lighter pattern, a sort of "orange peel" texture. The glaze pulls away from edges and corners well.

Franklin Textured Glaze

Dolomite	30%	
Potash feldspar	30	
Albany slip clay	20	
Ball clay	10	
Barium	10	
Iron oxide	8	

A very lively glaze. Where thick, it is a streaky dark to light ochre; where thin, a caramel, "orange peel" texture. The glaze pulls away from edges and corners.

Nichols Textured Glaze

Cedar Heights Redart	38%	
Dolomite	36	
Ball clay	18	
Bone ash	6	
Lithium carbonate	2	

A rich, almost heavy-looking textured glaze with an "orange peel" texture.

Harpersfield Textured Glaze

Cedar Heights Redart	40%	This glaze has a rich, deep color and an "orange peel" texture. The color varies from a heavy iron red to a translucent caramel.
Dolomite	32	
Ball clay	20	
Bone ash	6	
Lithium carbonate	2	
Iron oxide	8	

Turnwood Soft Green Glaze

Albany slip clay	30%	This glaze, where thick, is a lovely, soft, iron green. Where thin it is straw yellow in color.
Dolomite	28	
Potash feldspar	24	
Barium carbonate	10	
Ball clay	8	

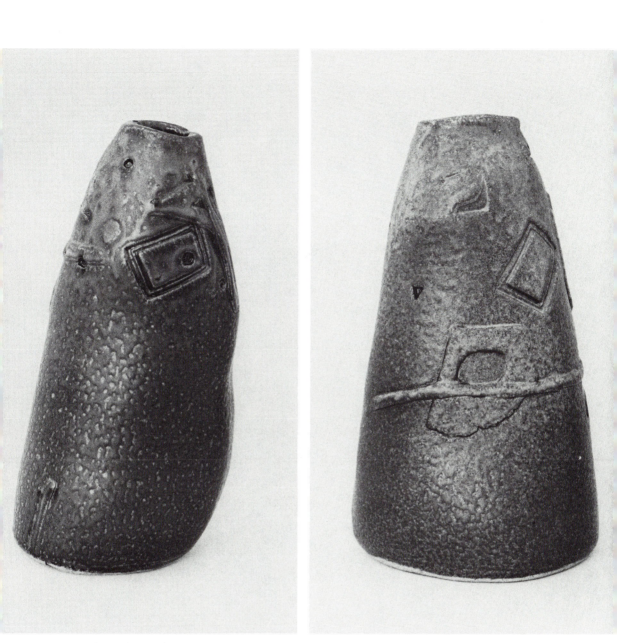

4-29   Richard Zakin. Oswego, New York. Cone 9. An example of Franklin Textured glaze.

4-30   Richard Zakin. Oswego, New York. Cone 9. A piece glazed with the Turnwood base and the Franklin Textured formula.

4-31   Richard Zakin. Oswego, New
York. Cone 9. A piece glazed with
Franklin Textured formula.

5 *Nonvitreous Surfaces*

Although it is a usual practice to finish ceramic work with a coating of vitreous glaze, slip, or engobe, other options are available, such as nonvitreous stains, slips, and engobes. These dull mat surfaces, with their strong, claylike texture, are particularly effective when used with sculptural pieces, whose surfaces are often so complex that they do not work well with glazes.

Stains

A stain is a transparent material that, when rubbed into a textured surface, darkens it and emphasizes its structure. On smooth surfaces, stains tend to look dull and uninteresting.

Many standard ceramic colorants work very well as stains. These include red and black iron oxide, cobalt oxide, chrome oxide, and manganese oxide. Be careful using the last two, as both are somewhat toxic (see page 220).

Prepared stains are available commercially. Although fairly expensive, they are much safer than colorants and offer a much greater breadth of color.

Certain clays, because they contain a high percentage of colorant as an impurity, also may be used as stains. Barnard clay and Albany slip clay give beautiful results when used as stains.

Stains may be used alone, for a dry mat effect, or with glazes and slips.

Bistre Stain

Cedar Heights Redart	50%	*A deep umber.*
Barnard slip clay	50	

Doku Brown Stain

Barnard slip clay	33%	*A rich, mottled brown.*
Wood ash	33	
Borax	34	

Barnard Stain

Barnard slip clay	90%	*An umber brown.*
Wollastonite	10	

Sanguine Stain

Cedar Heights Redart	100%	*A brick red.*

KE I Black Stain

Barnard slip clay	100%	
Cobalt oxide	3	
—*a blue-black*		

KE II Black Stain

Albany slip clay	100%
Cobalt oxide	1
Iron oxide	4
Manganese	2
Rutile	1

—a strong black

KE III Black Stain

Albany slip clay	100%
Cobalt oxide	4
Iron oxide	3
Rutile	0.5

—a strong blue-black

Iron/Rutile Stain

Iron oxide	50%
Rutile	50

5-1 William Hall. High Wycombe, Buckinghamshire, England. Cone 9.

5-2   William Hall. High Wycombe, Buckinghamshire, England. Cone 9.

5-3 Hans Coper. London, England. Cone 9. Coper employed a white slip and a dark manganese stain in a multilayer application procedure to produce the rich texture on the surface of this piece. *Courtesy of the Everson Museum, Syracuse, N.Y.*

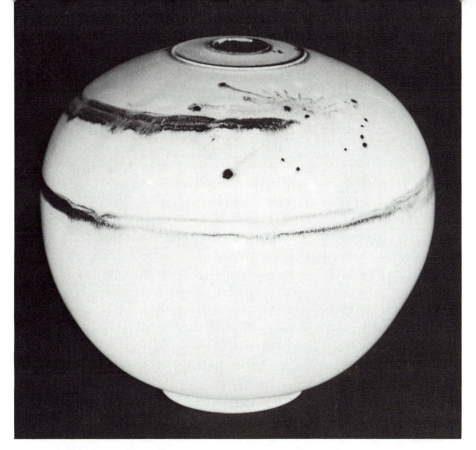

5-4 Judith Weber. New Rochelle, New York. Cone 7. This piece was decorated with iron, rutile, and black underglaze stain while still in the greenware state. After bisque firing, it was glazed with a formula that produced a translucent, soft gray glaze that works well with underglaze stains. This sort of manipulation is appropriate in the oxidation fire.

5-5 Richard Zakin. Oswego, New York. *Platter*. Cone 6. Handbuilt. A platter decorated in the Tzu Chou style. The KE II stain was applied to the piece, and sgraffito decoration cut with a scratchboard tool. The piece was then covered with volcanic ash clear glaze.

5-6 Ann Mortimer. Newmarket,
Ontario. Cone 9. The simplicity of
the form contrasts nicely with the
rough-textured, sand-blasted
surface. The piece is finished with a
thin slip.

156

Slips and Engobes

Slips and engobes use the same raw materials as glazes. They differ from each other only in their clay-to-nonclay ratios. Both slips and engobes are high in clay, slips having the highest amount of clay. Slips are mixtures whose clay content is 50 percent or more clay; engobes are mixtures whose clay content ranges from 25 to 50 percent. This high clay content produces formulas that are stable and do not run or blur in the fire.

Some potters feel that glazes run or blur from the great heat inside the kiln. This is because many overfired glazes run and blur even more than normal. But heat is only one cause of the problem. Another cause is the amount of alumina in the glaze. A high clay glaze, with its generous alumina content, will run and blur very little if at all, for alumina imparts viscosity and stiffness to the formula.

Slips and engobes are very compatible with other surface finishes. They may be used under glazes or with glazes, fluxes, or stains. Their character is also compatable with the oxidation fire, for both share a simplicity and clarity of effect.

SLIPS

These formulas vary in clay content (generally from 50 to 100 percent). They are stable, durable, and do not run or blur in the fire.

Slips may be applied when the clay is wet, dry, or bisque fired. Slips applied to wet clay generally have a soft, natural character; slips applied to dry clay or bisque-fired clay tend to have a precise, controlled character.

If the slip is applied to a wet clay body, its clay content should be normal, uncalcined clay. If it is applied to dry or bisque-fired clay, most of the clay content should be calcined. To calcine clay, place it in a bowl (unfired or bisque fired) and fire the clay to bisque. It will lose its water content and its plasticity; it will be dry, powdery, and nonshrinking. This last factor is very important, for it ensures a good fit between slips and dry or bisque-fired clay, both of which have already shrunk a great deal.

GRITTY SLIPS

Slips usually are made from smooth clays and sieved before they are used, so that the resulting texture is smooth and creamy. But if some of the clays used in the formula are coarse and the slip is not strained, the result will be a coarse, sandy-textured surface, which although not practical for functional pieces that must be clean and smooth (such as table ware) is appropriate for sculptural pieces.

Gritty slip formulas are simple mixtures of a few clays and perhaps a little flux. These slips may be applied by dipping, splashing, spraying, or brushing. They also may be applied in a graphic, painterly manner, in which case they

5-7 Barbara Frey. Commerce, Texas. Cone 6. Frey employs a very interesting method for applying slip to a clay slab. She applies trailed slip to a sheet of newspaper and then presses the clay slab on the newspaper. The result is imagery with a kind of printed quality. *Photo by Paul Pierce*

5-8   Barbara Frey. Commerce,
Texas. Cone 6. *Photo by Paul Pierce*

5-9   Barbara Frey. Commerce,
Texas. Cone 6. *Photo by Paul Pierce*

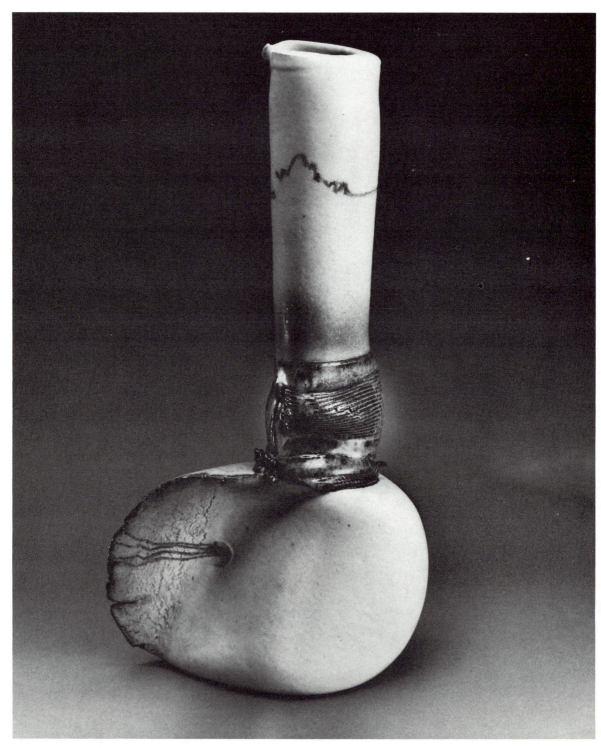

5-10 Louise Baldinger. Schenectady, New York. Cone 9. *Photo by Richard Baldinger*

will have characteristics similar to sand painting. They may be applied to greenware or bisque-fired ware. They may be used alone or in conjunction with stains and glazes.

Gritty slips are reliable and easy to use. When fired, they are surprisingly strong and resistant to abrasion, although they look soft and sandy.

ENGOBES

Engobes have a clay content higher than glazes but lower than slips, varying from 25 to 50 percent.

Engobes are best applied to dry greenware or to bisque-fired pieces.

Cone 3 Nonvitreous Surfaces

ENGOBES

Thendara I Engobe
(for application to wet clay)

Kaolin	46%
Talc	28
Opax	12
Gerstley borate	8
Barium carbonate	2
Borax	2
Tin oxide	2

5-11   Claude Conover. Cleveland,
Ohio. Cone 7. Conover achieves a
rich textured surface with a strong
emphasis on the rough, earthy
character of his clay body. The
pieces are stamped and scored while
wet. When dry they are fired to
bisque. At this point a stain is
applied to the body to darken it. A
white engobe is then applied in the
interstices for contrast and richness.

5-12   Claude Conover. Cleveland, Ohio. Cone 7.

5-13   Claude Conover. Cleveland,
Ohio. *Three Stoneware Ceramics*.
Cone 7.

Thendara II

(for application on bone dry or bisque-fired clay)

Kaolin	10%	*This engobe is hard surfaced and durable.*
Calcined kaolin	36	*It can be used as a final surface finish or*
Talc	28	*as an underglaze slip. It may be colored*
Opax	12	*with the normal ceramic colorants or with*
Gerstley borate	8	*those stains that retain their color and*
Barium carbonate	2	*brilliance at cone 3.*
Borax	2	
Tin oxide	2	

Listed below is a sampling of colorant percentages and the fired result, for use with the Thendara I and II engobes.

1. cobalt oxide
    1% oxford cloth mid-blue
    2% dark blue
2. chrome oxide
    1% light green
    2% medium green
3. iron oxide
    3% cool gray
    6% iron (military) gray
4. cobalt/chrome
    1% cobalt oxide + 1% chrome oxide—turquoise

Cone 6 Nonvitreous Surfaces

GRITTY SLIPS

Ozona White

AP Green	70%	*Stony white.*
Cedar Heights Goldart	20	
Ball clay	10	

5-14 Richard Zakin. Oswego, New York. *Bowl*. Cone 6. Handbuilt. The piece was first dipped in Mouse Black and then partially in Corinth Blue Green. The imagery is an iron-rutile stain applied with brush and sponge.

166

Ozona Naples Yellow

AP Green	40%	*Light ochre.*
Cedar Heights Goldart	40	
Cedar Heights Redart	12	
Ball clay	6	
Wollastonite	2	

Ozona Red

AP Green	60%	*Brick red.*
Cedar Heights Goldart	15	
Cedar Heights Redart	25	

Ozona Burgundy

AP Green	80%
Cedar Heights Goldart	20
Chrome oxide	1
Iron oxide	2

   —deep brick red

Ozona Green Gray

AP Green	70%
Cedar Heights Goldart	20
Ball clay	10
Chrome oxide	3

   —light tan gray-green

Ozona Mid-Gray Green

AP Green	70%
Cedar Heights Goldart	20
Ball clay	10
Cobalt oxide	1
Chrome oxide	1

   —tan gray-green

Ozona Mid-Gray Blue

AP Green	70%
Cedar Heights Goldart	20
Ball clay	10
Cobalt oxide	1
Iron oxide	1

   —tan gray-blue

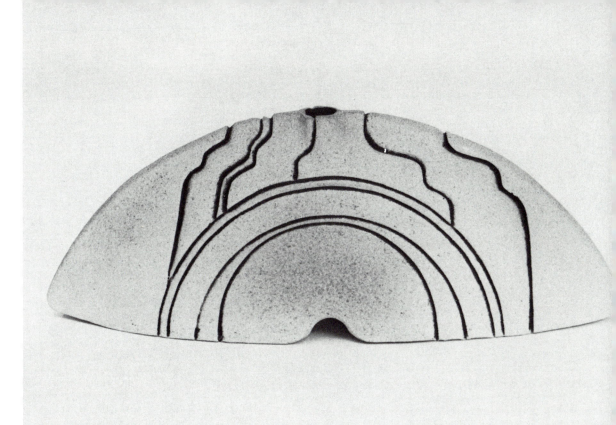

5-15   Richard Zakin. Oswego, New York. Cone 6. Although the gritty slips do not
work well with functional forms, they do seem to be consonant in character with
certain types of sculptured vessels.

5-16   Richard Zakin. Oswego, New York. *Vase.* Cone 6. Handbuilt. This piece was
dipped into gritty red slip and then bisque fired. Bistre stain was applied in the
interstices, and the piece was fired to maturity.

5-17   Richard Zakin. Oswego, New York. *Wall Hanging Vase*. Cone 6. Handbuilt.
Note the contrast of the hard-edged carving and the soft-looking gritty slip.

5-18   Richard Zakin. Oswego, New York. Cone 6. An example of a piece finished in
the Ozona White gritty slip, applied when the clay was still fairly wet. When the
piece dried, it was fired to bisque. At that point a dark Bistre stain was applied to the
stamped areas, and the piece was fired to maturity.

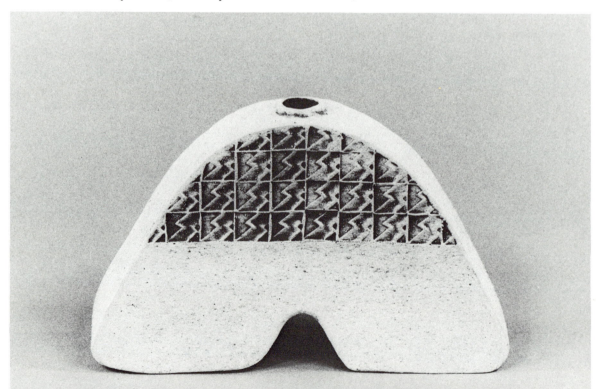

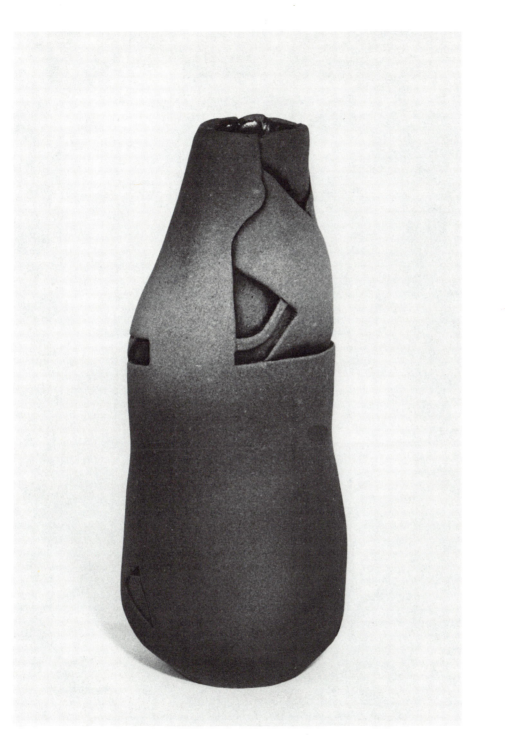

5-19   Richard Zakin. Oswego, New York. *Vase*. Cone 6. Handbuilt. This piece is covered with Ozona Blue gritty slip. At the center top there is a light spray of Ozona White gritty slip. The result is a soft modulation from blue to white.

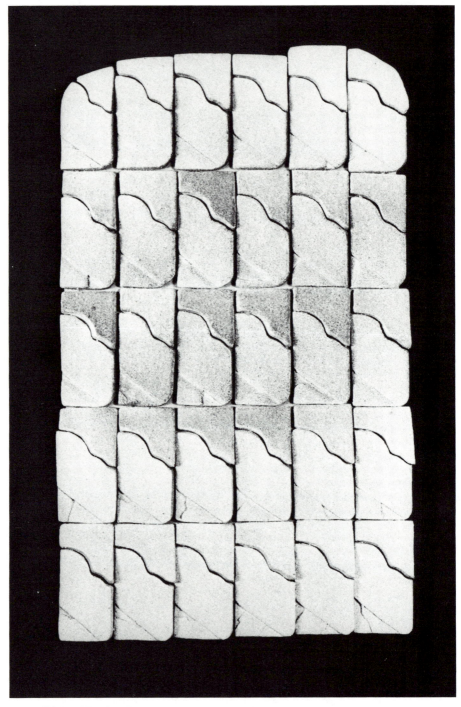

5-20 Richard Zakin. Oswego, New York. *Modular Tile Piece*. Cone 6. Handbuilt. In the greenware state, the tiles were sprayed with Ozona White gritty slip and with an overspray of Ozona Blue gritty slip. After bisque firing, Bistre stain was applied in the interstices, and the piece was fired to maturity.

172

ENGOBES

Fired slips and engobes are somewhat similar, but engobes tend to be more brilliant in color than slips. The Ontario Engobe is smooth, very mat, opaque, nonflowing, and durable.

Ontario Engobe

Nepheline syenite	25%	*This formula may be applied to unfired*
Kaolin	36	*pieces. To apply to bisque-fired pieces, half*
Flint	18	*the kaolin content (18 percent) should be*
Dolomite	10	*calcined.*
Frit 90 or 3124	6	
Zircopax	5	

Cone 9 Nonvitreous Surfaces

ENGOBES

Pilgrim I Engobe

(for application to dry or bisque-fired clay)

Kaolin	4%	*This engobe is hard-surfaced and durable.*
Calcined kaolin	48	*It can be used as a final surface or as an*
Talc	20	*underglaze material. It may be colored*
Opax	12	*with the normal ceramic colorants or with*
Potash feldspar	10	*those stains that retain their color when*
Borax	2	*fired to cone 9.*
Barium carbonate	2	
Tin oxide	2	

6 *Glaze Application*

It is difficult to convey to the beginning potter the problems associated with applying glaze to clay. The process is complicated and time-consuming. Often there is no sure way of predicting how the piece will turn out until it is removed from the kiln.

In painting, color and form are generally applied and delineated with a brush. In high-fire ceramics, the brush is only one glaze application tool among many (and indeed a tool often unjustly neglected). Dipping, pouring, and spraying are the most common methods used for applying glaze.

In oxidation, high-fire glaze application is especially worthy of discussion, as oxidation offers many opportunities for the potter and makes many demands. Good glaze formulas are important but good glaze application is perhaps even more important. The oxidation fire demands concentration and attention to detail during the glaze application process.

Dipping

Of all the methods of glaze application, dipping is the simplest and most direct. This method, therefore, is probably the best introduction to glaze application. The potter simply dips the object to be glazed into a bucket of liquid glaze. A large amount of glaze must be mixed beforehand.

Glazing may be done with the object held by hand or with the aid of glaze tongs. If the object is hand held, one part is grasped firmly and the rest is lowered into the glaze bucket. The object is allowed to dry. Part of the section

174

6-1 John Chalke. Calgary, Alberta. *Platter.* Using a great variety of glazes and glaze application techniques, Chalke is able to achieve a very rich surface on his handbuilt platters.

already glazed is then grasped carefully, and the unglazed section of the object is immersed in the glaze. To make sure that the piece is completely glazed, it is necessary to overlap the glaze. This overlapped section looks quite different from the rest of the glaze in color and texture; it is stronger in color and more opaque.

In cases where the potter wishes to avoid this glaze overlap, glaze tongs may be used. Glaze tongs are plierlike devices that enable the potter to dip entire pieces into the glaze bucket in one operation. The tongs will leave tiny unglazed marks or spots behind, which can be filled with a brush. Before glazing, practice with the tongs to learn to dip them smoothly and slowly into and out of the bucket. The tongs must be moved slowly to avoid drips and runs. If employed correctly, glaze tongs leave no evidence of their use. Be forewarned, however, that pieces weighing over fifteen or twenty pounds are difficult to dip with tongs; it is better to spray large pieces than to attempt to dip them.

Splashing and Pouring

In this method of glaze application, the potter pours or splashes glaze over the object. This results in a glaze with many thickness variations. Color variations are similar to those achieved in the dipping process; in this case, however, the glaze modulations are softer and irregular.

The potter needs to prepare only a small amount of glaze; a catch basin is placed below the object, and glaze is carefully poured over the object. The excess glaze that has run into the catch basin may be reused.

This method can be used alone or in combination with dipping and spraying, as shown.

Intaglio Glazing

In intaglio glazing, the potter daubs glaze into the textured areas of the bisqued piece and then sponges the surface so that the glaze remains only in the interstices (crevices) of the form. This heightens the contrast between the textured and untextured areas of the piece and enriches its surface.

Intaglio glazing is a two-stage process. The textures are pressed, stamped, scratched, or carved into the clay when the piece is formed or soon after; glaze is applied after the piece is bisque fired. This method is simple and reliable, allowing much variety and freedom of imagery.

Intaglio glazing can be used alone or in combination with dipping, splashing, or spraying. It is especially appropriate for use with sculpture and sculptural pottery.

6-2 Immersing the hand-held pot.

6-3 Glaze tongs in use.

6-4 If the piece is dipped smoothly, in one operation, no glaze overlap will occur.

6-5   Richard Zakin. Oswego, New York. *Plate*. Cone 6. Handbuilt. This piece was dipped into the Wollastonite II glaze (no colorant). It was then dipped into Mouse Black with a narrow band left in reserve. The lighter colored section of the plate is the section that was not covered with Mouse Black glaze.

6-6   Richard Zakin. Oswego, New York. *Wall Hanging Vase*. Cone 6. Handbuilt. This piece was first dipped into Gritty Red slip, then the bottom part into Gritty White slip while still in the greenware state. It was then fired to bisque, and the Bistre stain was applied to the carved areas.

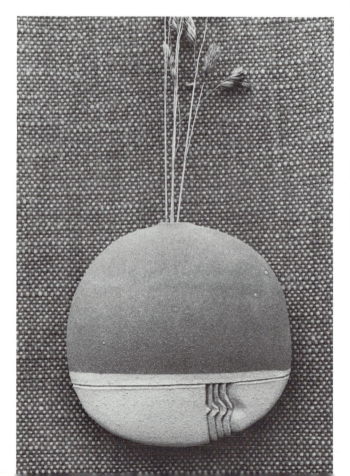

6-7 In this illustration of splash glazing, the platter has already been prepared by an application of GK white glaze over the whole piece. Now a colored glaze is splashed in an irregular fashion over part of the piece.

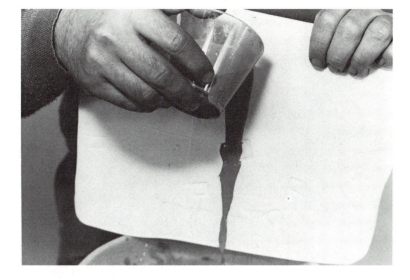

6-8 Marylyn Dintenfass. Mamaroneck, New York. *Cup*. Cone 9. Handbuilt. The splashed image (a cobalt blue glaze applied to a white glaze over porcelain) beautifully complements the billowing forms, which serve as a sort of handle for this piece.

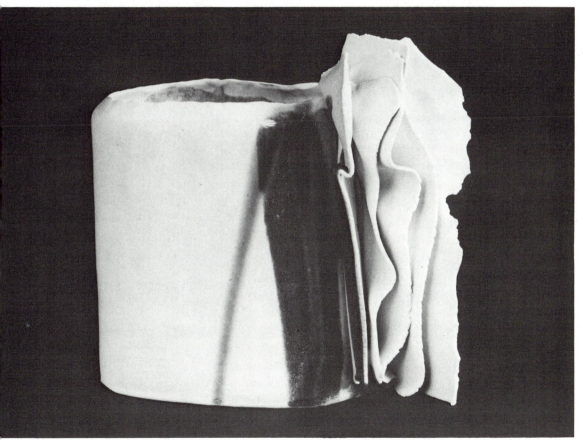

179

6-9 Ian Auld. *Vase*. Cone 9.
Handbuilt. Splashed and poured
glaze can produce a very harsh
image. Here, however, Auld creates
a soft, rich effect by splashing with
grayed, earth-toned blues and tans,
which are quite close in value.

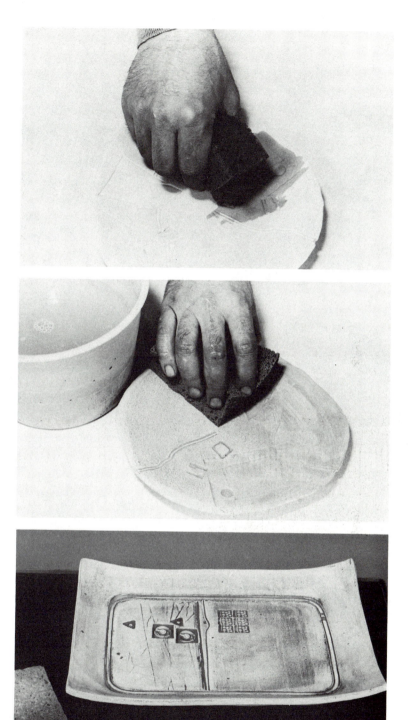

6-10 The potter daubs glaze or stain into the interstices.

6-11 The excess color is sponged away, leaving the color only in the interstices.

6-12 In this example, the glaze has been applied to the interstices and the piece is now ready for final glazing.

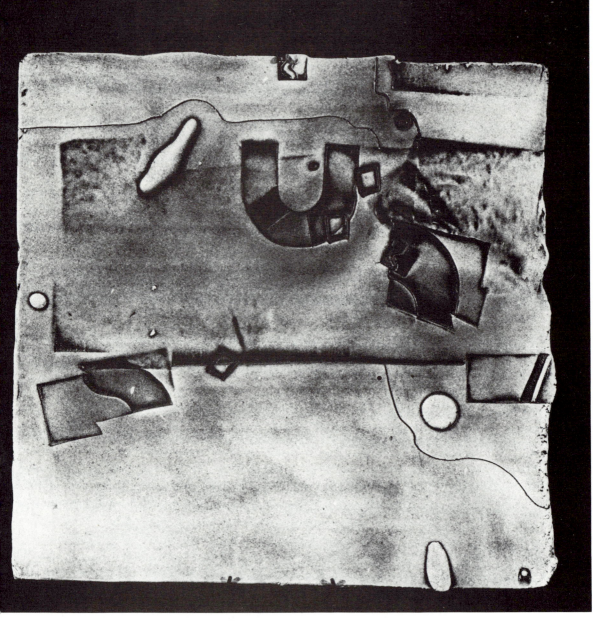

6-13 Richard Zakin. Oswego, New York.
Plaque. Cone 6. This piece was finished
using an intaglio glazing procedure. It was
first sprayed with Ozona White gritty slip
while still wet. When dry it was fired to
bisque. The Mouse Black glaze was
daubed in the interstices in an intaglio
procedure. The overall effect is
reminiscent of a softground etching.

6-14   Louise Baldinger.
Schenectady, New York.
Covered Jar. Cone 9.
Handbuilt. The impressed
imagery in this piece has been
emphasized by the application
of a black glaze in the
interstices. The intaglio
procedure can be used to
emphasize the richness of
imagery impressed in the clay.

6-15   Louise Baldinger.
Schenectady, New York.
Covered Jar. Cone 9.
Handbuilt.

6-16   Richard Zakin. Oswego, New
York. *Bowl.* Cone 6. Handbuilt.
Mouse Black was applied to the
incised areas, and then the piece
was splashed with Wollastonite II
glaze (no colorant). Finally it was
dipped into a clear wood ash glaze.

Tzu Chou Black Slip Decoration

This method used in decorating clay in its greenware state was developed by Chinese potters during the Sung dynasty and is still in use today. The many variations that comprise the Tzu Chou technique all rely on the use of non-running, high clay glazes. Many of the dark glazes used by Chinese potters working in Tzu Chou styles can be duplicated today using glazes composed largely of Albany slip clay.

The most common Tzu Chou technique involves the use of a dark slip over a light body; the design is scratched through the slip to the body. A variation involves the use of a light slip over a dark body; here again a design is scratched through the slip to the body. This type of decoration enables the potter to obtain intricate, graphic imagery. Tzu Chou pottery is usually fired once.

Brush Decoration

In most stoneware glazes, the brush is used best as a tool for applying linear imagery rather than broad areas of glaze. No matter how neatly broad areas of most glazes are applied, they will reveal after firing a fussy texture of brush marks. Smooth, unbroken surfaces are very common in the oxidation fire. It is just this sort of glaze surface that is most appropriate as a background for linear imagery.

Brushes and brush techniques vary. Much experimentation is required to find out what brushes will do when used to apply ceramic glazes and stains. The Chinese or Japanese bamboo brush gives a soft, sinuous line. The Japanese hake, a flat, soft-bristle brush, gives a much wider line that is beautiful both when charged with glaze and when used in a dry-brush technique. Sign-writer's brushes give a thin, controlled line. House-painter's brushes (especially old ones) give an interesting textured effect.

Spraying

Glazes fired in oxidation are often contrasty and harsh in appearance. One of the best ways to enrich the glaze surfaces of oxidation-fired ceramics is with the spray method of glaze application. A simple procedure is to dip or splash a base color on the object and then spray a second color over this.

Most of my students fire their work in the oxidation kiln. We have struggled for many years to work out glazing procedures that would enable students firing in oxidation to achieve the richness and subtlety available to their fellow students firing in reduction. This had to be achieved reliably, with reasonably simple methods. The combination of dipping and spraying has proven successful and seems to have answered many of our problems.

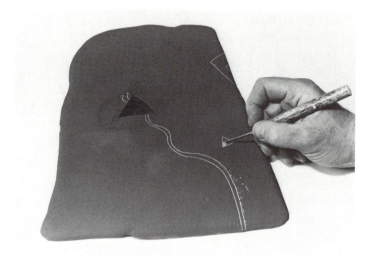

6-17 In this example of Tzu Chou decoration, the piece has been covered with a black slip. The design is then carved through the dark slip to the light-colored clay.

6-18 Richard Zakin. Oswego, New York. *Plate*. Handbuilt. Here the Mouse Black glaze was applied to bisque fired clay rather than greenware. The imagery was cut with a dental tool rather than a scratchboard tool. The linear imagery has a crisp, engraved character.

6-19   Pat Wynne and Richard Zakin.
Plate. Cone 6. Tzu Chou decoration.
Wynne is an illustrator of children's books
and scientific subjects; her work is noted
for its delicacy and keen observation. The
author formed the plate and applied the
glaze. Wynne drew on the piece. It was
then fired to maturity. The Tzu Chou
techniques offer wonderful opportunities
for partnerships between potters and other
artists.

6-20 Edwin and Mary Scheier. Green
Valley, Arizona. Cone 8/9. The striking
drawing in this piece was cut through the
dark glaze to the lighter clay body. This
sort of linear imagery has been a great
specialty of the Scheiers since the late
1930s.

6-21 Edwin and Mary
Scheier. Green Valley,
Arizona.

6-22 Edwin and Mary
Scheier. Green Valley,
Arizona.

6-23 Edwin and Mary Scheier. Green Valley, Arizona. Cone 8/9. *From the collection of Muriel and Martin Barzelay*

6-24 Edwin and Mary Scheier. Detail of Figure 6-23.

6-25 Wayne Bates. Murray, Kentucky. Cone 6. Bates is a production potter who has worked out an elegant technique for oxidation work. Colored slips are applied to the piece. It is then sprayed with wax and allowed to dry for two days. A design is then carved into the slip to the white fineclay body. The piece is bisque fired, and a clear or mat cone 6 glaze applied over the piece, at which point it is fired to cone 6.

6-26 Wayne Bates. Murray, Kentucky. Cone 6.

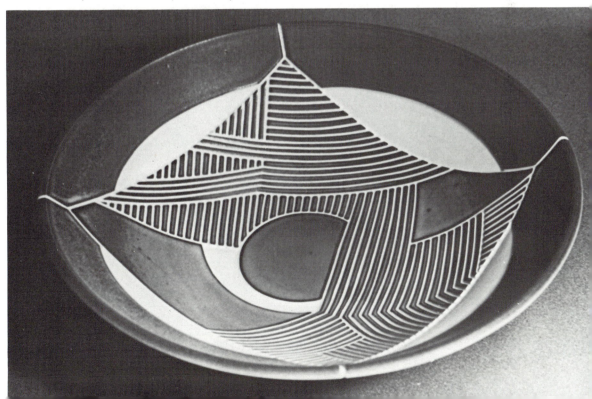

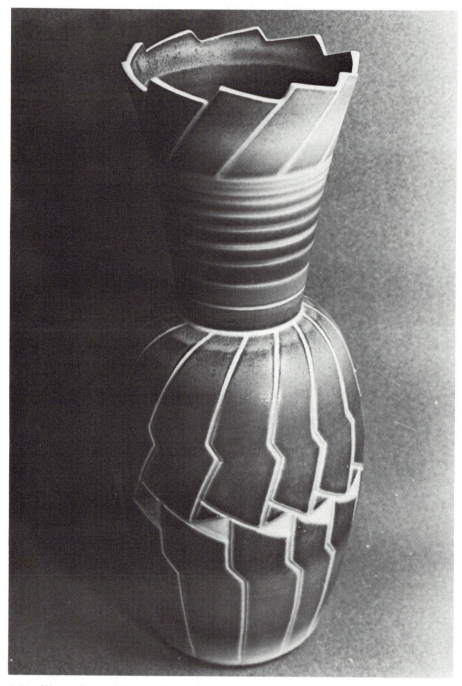

6-27 Wayne Bates. Murray, Kentucky. Cone 6.

6-28 Lucie Rie. London, England. Cone 9. Porcelain. In these pieces the glazes are applied with a brush on greenware. On one part of the piece or another Rie carves or scratches through the glaze into the porcelain clay body. Occasionally she will then brush another glaze over this carving. In this way she builds up a complex, rich imagery.

6-29 Lucie Rie. London, England. Cone 9. Porcelain.

6-30   Mathias Osterman. Toronto, Ontario. Cone 9.

6-31   Mathias Osterman. Toronto, Ontario. Cone 9.

6-32 Decorating with a brush and atomizer-sprayer. A smooth, white mat glaze has been applied to the plate. Imagery is applied using Mouse Black slip glaze.

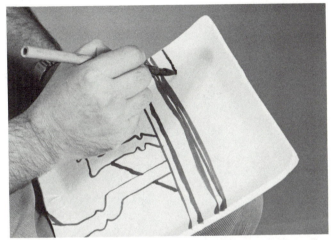

6-33 The drawing process.

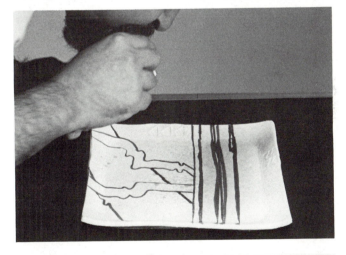

6-34 A light spray of thin Mouse Black glaze is applied to part of the plate.

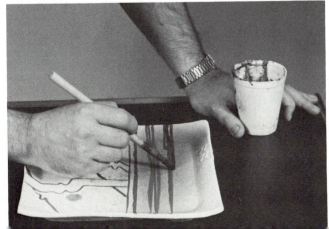

6-35 Drawing back into the sprayed area.

6-36   Richard Zakin. Oswego, New York. Cone 6. The color range of this piece is limited to black, gray, and white, which gave me great freedom to deal with a complicated imagery.

6-37 Kevin Byrne. Tulsa, Oklahoma. The patterns in these production pieces are drawn over a white tin glaze and then fired to cone 4. Byrne feels that there are potters "who would like to go further than simply letting the glaze do all the decorating." He is obviously one of these potters himself.

6-38 Kevin Byrne. Tulsa, Oklahoma.

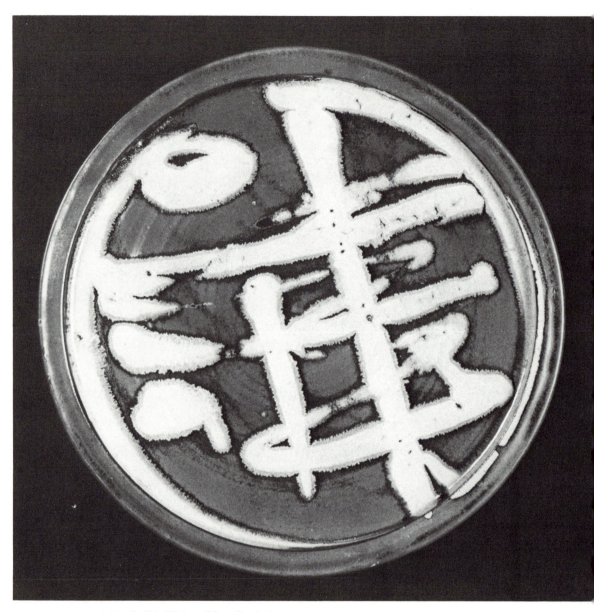

6-39 Judith Weber. New Rochelle, New York. Cone 7. Weber uses two glazes and a wax-resist technique to achieve a rich imagery. A base glaze is applied, an image (often calligraphic, as in this piece) is painted over the base glaze, and a contrasting and textured glaze is applied. *Photo by Robert L. Weber*

6-40 Dorothy Hafner. New York, New York. *Synapse I*. Cone 6. Hafner says of her work: "In New York City, where I choose to live and work, fuel firing is neither safe nor healthy. Oxidation firing (in the electric kiln) is not only suitable for my urban life but preferable in terms of the decorative focus of my work. My chosen palette as a painter was toward rich color juxtapositions. In ceramics, in which I now work, the pastels and high-chroma colors I want are only achieved in oxidation. Though these colors are also easily achieved at lower temperatures (I fire cone 6 porcelain), I like the strength, ring, and texture of the higher fired ware. Because my recent work is designed for use at the table, a high-fired body is, of course, more suitable than porous earthenwares, which can absorb stains where the raw clay remains exposed."
Photo by Malcolm Varon

6-41 Dorothy Hafner. New York,
New York. Cone 6.

200

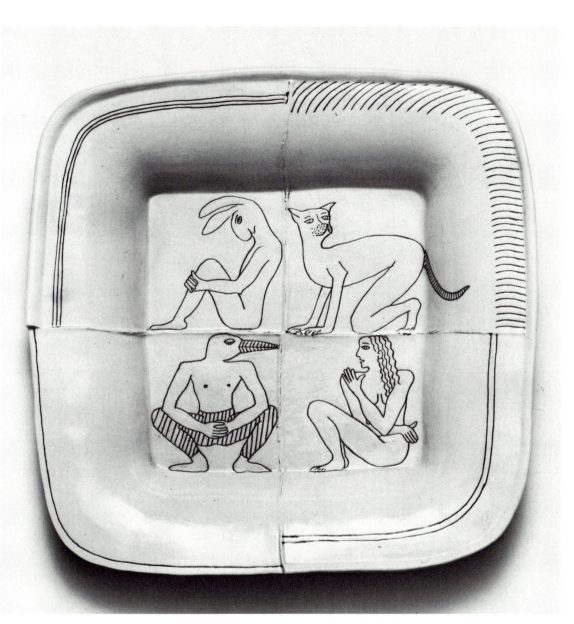

6-42 Alison Britton. London,
England. *Platter*. Britton uses a thin,
wiry, clay inlay technique to create a
graphic image of great clarity.

6-43 Alison Britton. London, England. *Pitcher*. Clay inlay and underglaze stain imagery. *Photo by David Cripps*

6-44 Alison Britton. London, England. *Rabbit Picture Plaque*. Clay inlay imagery. *Photo by David Cripps*

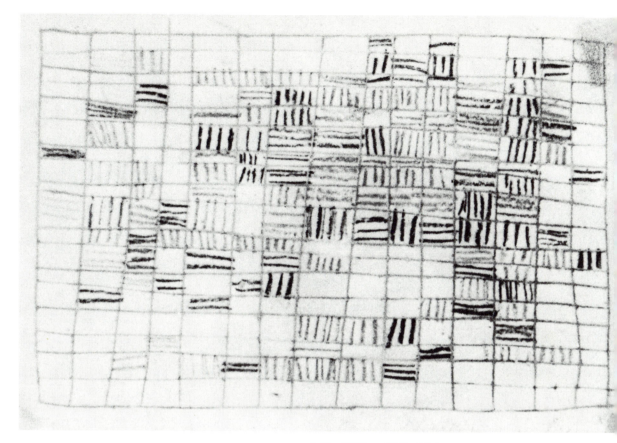

6-45   William Hall. High
Wycombe, Buckinghamshire,
England. Cone 9. This piece is
drawn not with a brush but with a
glaze pencil.

6-46 Richard Zakin.
Oswego, New York. Cone 6.
Mouse Black was drawn on
bisque-fired white fineclay
using a draftsman's pen. The
piece was then fired to
maturity.

6-47 Maryanne Cain.
Toronto, Ontario. Cone 6.
Though this piece has the
durability of stoneware, the
color and imagery are
reminiscent of low-fire work.

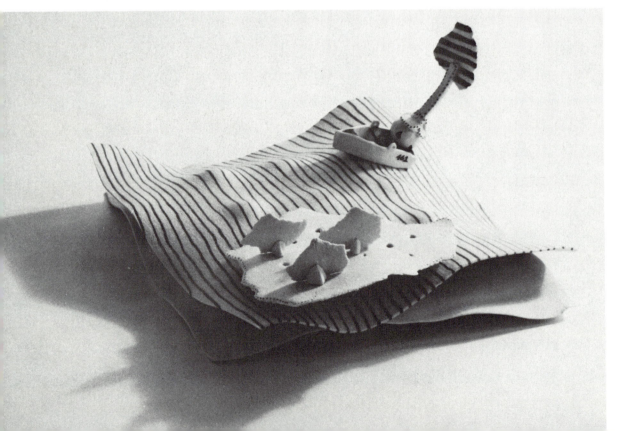

6-48 Mutsuo Yanagihara.
Kyoto, Japan. *Memory Of Sky
II*. Cone 9. Yanagihara has
worked on a series of pieces
related to this theme in a
technique that owes much to
the low fire.

6-49 Sally Ann Endleman. New Haven,
Connecticut. Endleman employs a wax-
resist technique. She paints on the bisque-
fired piece with a commercially prepared
liquid wax that is used as a wax resist. She
then dips the piece in the glaze. The light
body contrasts with the dark glaze.

6-50 Sally Ann Endleman. New Haven,
Connecticut.

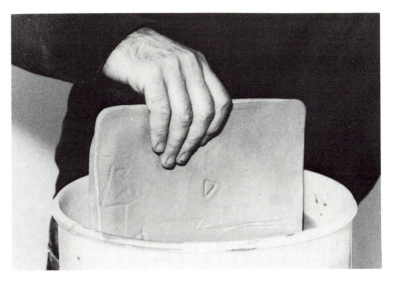

6-51 Dipping and spraying a platter. Here the piece is dipped into G.K. white.

6-52 After the white glaze is dry, it is sprayed with a light coat of Brutus Blue.

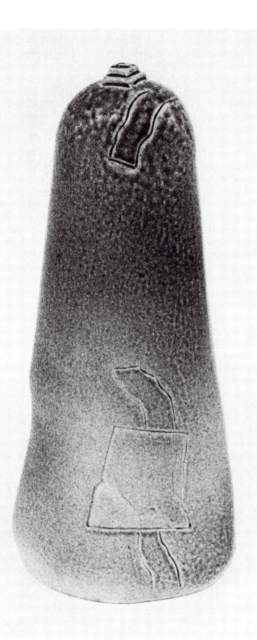

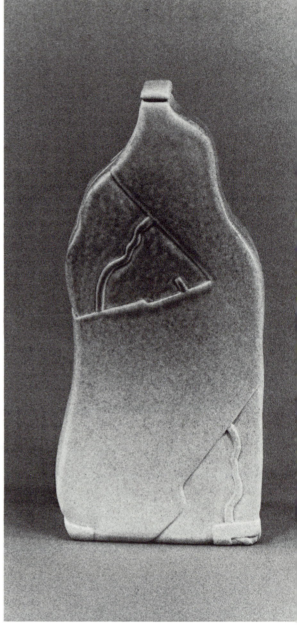

6-53   Richard Zakin. Oswego, New York. *Vase.* Cone 6. Handbuilt. Spraying softens the transition from one glaze color to another. This piece was sprayed with G.K. white and Corinth Blue. Then the shoulder of the piece was sprayed with a heavy application of Brutus Blue (a textured glaze).

6-54   Richard Zakin. Oswego, New York. Cone 6. Here, too, the sprayed modulation of one glaze to another is an important aspect of the fired piece.

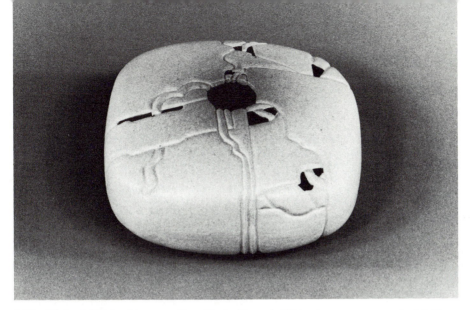

6-55   Richard Zakin. Oswego, New York. Cone 6. This piece was sprayed with Troy white glaze. The same glaze base, with 1 percent cobalt oxide added for color, was then sprayed on the shoulder and lip of the piece.

6-56   Richard Zakin. Oswego, New York. Cone 6. This piece was sprayed overall with a white glaze, Troy base, and the same base with 1 percent cobalt added to make blue.

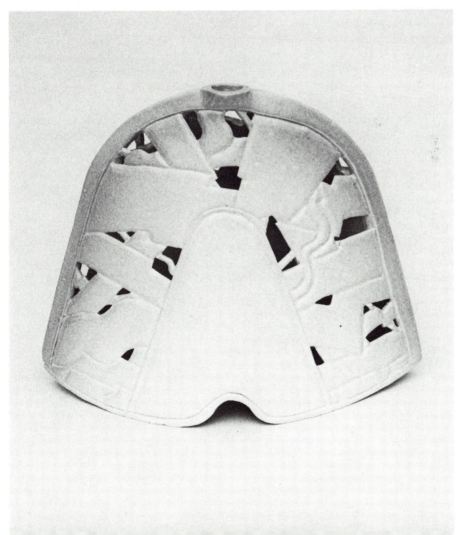

THE ATOMIZER-SPRAYER

The atomizer-sprayer has two pipes that together form an L. The bottom pipe (the long end) is placed in the liquid to be sprayed; the top pipe (the short end) is placed in the mouth. Air is blown through the short pipe, causing a weak vacuum to form at the top of the long pipe. The liquid at the bottom of the long pipe is drawn up and then sprayed out. This simple machine is a useful leftover from another era. It is quiet, reliable, inexpensive, and portable. It is not as convenient for big jobs as other sprayers, but it is very good for small jobs and for decoration.

The atomizer-sprayer has one serious drawback: it is not as safe as other sprayers. Many potters have become aware of the health hazards related to their work. If the potter sprays toxic materials, such as barium, or sprays a large number of pieces, the sprayer-atomizer is not appropriate; dangerous materials may be absorbed into the lungs. For occasional spraying, however, or as an introduction to the spraying process, this is a most useful tool.

THE PAASCHE MODEL L SPRAYER

The Paasche Model L sprayer is actually an oversized airbrush. It is a simple device with few controls, but it has two important advantages: it is extremely easy to use—it is highly immune to blockages even when it is used to spray unscreened materials—and it is easily cleaned and well made. This type of sprayer is called external mix; the air from the compressor and the liquid glaze do not mix inside the sprayer but rather at a point midway between the air and glaze nozzles. By this simple strategy, the weaknesses of most spray mechanisms are avoided and very few blockages occur. If there is a blockage, it is in the feed tube connected to the glaze container; since this tube is open and straight, it can be cleaned easily.

The sprayer requires very little air (25 p.s.i. will do) and is in the mid-price range for spraying units. It may be fitted with a wide nozzle at the top of the feed tube to accommodate rough, unscreened mixtures.

COMPRESSORS

There are two very different types of compressors. The first is used only with an airbrush; it is small, quiet, and very carefully made, but it is not a multi-purpose tool. The second is stronger, larger, and noisier; it is not as carefully built, but it has many uses. The small models are made by Paasche and DeVilbiss. The larger models are available from hardware outlets and stores like Sears. Both compressors work very well and can be recommended safely.

6-57 Using the atomizer-sprayer.

6-58 Maurice Savoie. Longueuil, Québec. Cone 9. Savoie works with porcelain bodies. His glazes are carefully formulated and applied to produce an evocative, strongly personal imagery.

6-59 Maurice Savoie.
Longueuil, Québec. Cone 9.

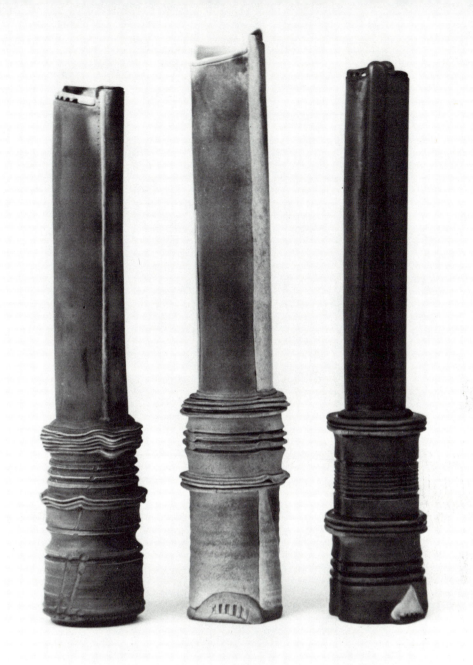

6-60 Kathryn Dennison.
Rochester, New York. Cone 6.
These pieces were sprayed with
water-soluble colorants, such as
cobalt and iron sulfate. These
soluble stains have a rich character.
They must, however, be carefully
used, as the soluble colorants are
quite toxic. Once they are fired,
they are safe for the user.

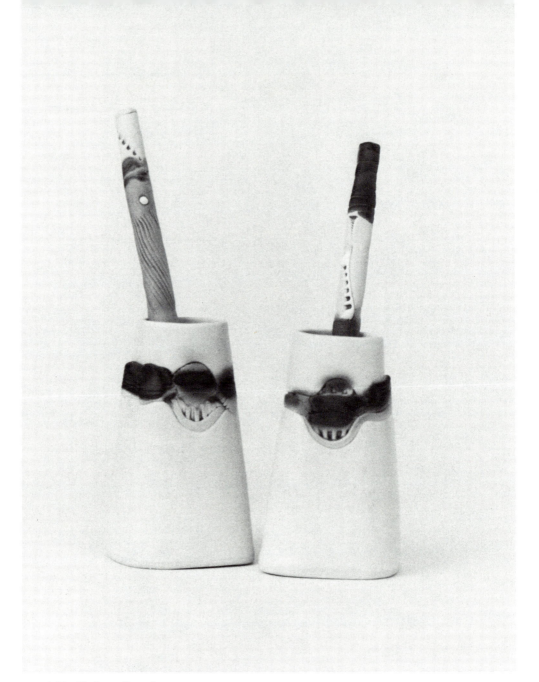

6-61 Kathryn Dennison.
Rochester, New York. *Cups with clay
straws.* Cone 6. Handbuilt pressed
imagery with colored clays and
sprayed soluble stains.

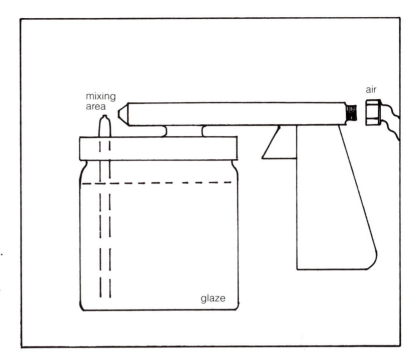

6-62 An external mix sprayer. This sprayer has a simple, foolproof construction. The mixing area can be especially troublesome on most sprayers, for it is usually buried in the mechanism. In this type, the mixing area is completely open. Blockages rarely occur.

6-63 I have substituted my own container and harness for the supplied container. Although mine doesn't look as finished and isn't as jostleproof, it allows me to change glaze containers quickly and easily.

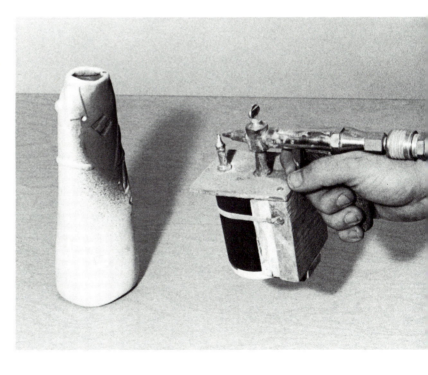

AN IRON SPRAY TECHNIQUE

This technique has two significant advantages: (1). Stamped and carved images are shown to good advantage, for this is a stain technique. (2). What you see before you fire looks like the final product. This is important to potters who do not like the transformation that glazes undergo in the kiln.

The procedure is simple. First, a glaze is rubbed into the interstices of the bisque-fired form; the form is then sponged so that the glaze remains in the interstices (the intaglio method). A thin solution of iron oxide and water is then sprayed over the form. Variations can be produced by concentrating the stain in one area. At this point the stain may be burnished with a soft cloth. The form is now ready for firing.

In one variation of this technique, a light or white glaze is sprayed over the smoothed iron stain. G.K. white is especially good for this.

Applying Wood Ash Glazes

Wood ash glazes may be applied by dipping, pouring, brushing, or spraying. Unfortunately, most spray guns block up when used to spray the coarse particles of wood ash glazes. Two remedies are available: the wood ash may be screened or, even better, ball milled. Both screening and ball milling soften the texture of wood ash glazes, giving an interesting variation. Normal, fairly coarse wood ash glazes may be sprayed in the Paasche model L sprayer, which has an almost unblockable external mix configuration. Always wear a mask when spraying wood ash glazes.

Because the texture of wood ash glazes is strongly patterned, certain other textures in the glaze tend to blur. Consequently, a glaze may be applied successfully over a large area if it has a generous wood ash content. Experiment on test tiles or test pieces before proceeding with a valuable piece.

Testing Glazes

To test a glaze formula, you need two plastic buckets, a rubber scraper, a small gram scale, and an 80- or 100-mesh nonrusting sieve.

One hundred grams of a glaze is the usual amount made up for testing. If you make less than 100 grams, your measurements may be inaccurate. Most formulas are written so that, aside from the colorants, they add up to 100 grams.

Weigh the materials, placing them as they are weighed into a plastic bucket. Stir the mixture thoroughly. Then add enough water so that the glaze is as thin as milk. Place a sieve on top of a second plastic bucket and pour the mixture through the sieve.

Label a test tile made from a *known* clay body. (Never test an unknown clay body and an unknown glaze together; always test an unknown with a known.) Wax over the label to protect it, and dip or spray the glaze on the tile.

6-64 Richard Zakin. Oswego, New York.
A piece finished with an iron stain.

6-65 Richard Zakin. Oswego, New York.
An example of iron stain technique.

6-66 Richard Zakin.
Oswego, New York. *Platter*.
Cone 6. Handbuilt. Mouse
Black was applied to the
crevices and the piece dipped
into transparent wood ash
glaze. Iron oxide was sprayed
over the glaze and the piece
fired to maturity.

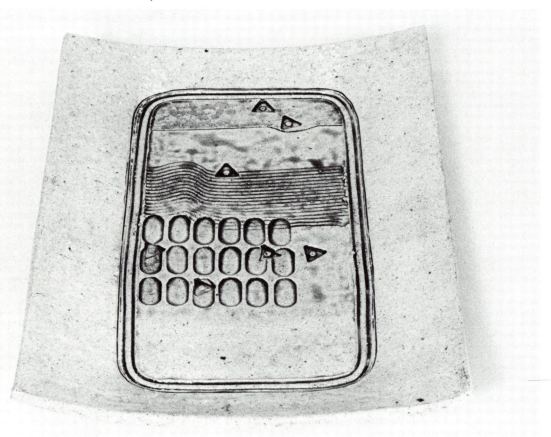

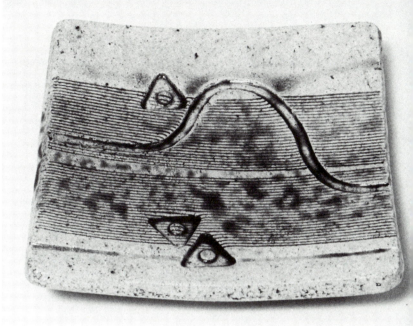

6-67 Richard Zakin. Oswego, New York. Cone 6. Mouse Black slip glaze was applied to the interstices on the surface of the piece and a clear, straw-colored wood ash glaze applied.

6-68 Richard Zakin. *Platter.* Cone 6. Handbuilt. Mouse Black glaze was applied to the indented areas. Then a thin coating of the same glaze was splashed on the bottom half of the platter. The piece was then dipped in a dark-colored, transparent wood ash glaze and fired to maturity.

Testing Glaze Bases

To test a glaze base to see how it will react with various colorants, mix 500 grams of the glaze. While it is dry, mix it *extremely* thoroughly. You may sieve it with a 30- or 50-mesh screen, which will mix the glaze well; if you use this method, wear a mask, for in dry sieving you may breath dangerous dusts. Once thoroughly dry mixed, divide the 500 grams into five different lots. Four will be tested with colorants; the last will be tested as a glaze base without colorants.

Because of losses from sieving, the last lot will probably not weigh 100 grams; it is therefore best to leave it without colorants. Apply the glaze either by dipping or spraying. Use a clay with which you are familiar. At least two of your colorant combinations also should be ones with which you are familiar. Label all test tiles and all glaze containers carefully.

If the glaze looks good on the test, try it on a larger form. Use it on a piece that is typical of your work, and apply it in a way similar to your normal application methods.

Safety Procedures

A number of glaze ingredients are somewhat toxic (the colorants powdered manganese dioxide and chrome green oxide, for example); care should be taken when using them. The following suggestions are simple, rational, and easily followed.

When mixing the glaze, wear an effective dust mask; wear gloves or wash your hands thoroughly after they are immersed in the glaze.

When applying the glaze, wear a smock or change clothing after glazing. If the glaze is applied by spraying, wear a dust mask.

After glazing wash carefully and vacuum the studio.

If your studio is equipped with a ventilation fan—and it should be—turn it on during the mixing, application, and clean-up procedures.

Keeping Notes

I require all my students to keep a notebook. The student draws each piece before it is glazed and then describes the glaze procedures. When the student or other students wish to achieve a similar effect, the notes are very useful. If the piece is exhibited in one of our exhibition cases, the description is transferred to a small card and placed next to the piece.

This one step has had more positive influence on my students' glazing than anything else I can think of.

Students are asked to write an evaluation of each piece in their notebooks immediately after the glaze description. Students are encouraged to draw and describe other students' successful glazed pieces. They are also asked to keep notes on the individual glazes they work with and describe their characteristics.

This kind of record keeping would be useful to any potter. It encourages the potter to learn from experience.

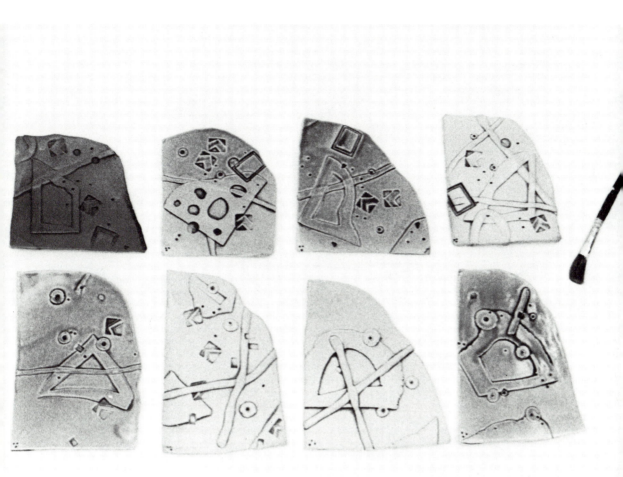

6-69 These large glaze tests (15–20 centimeters tall) are fired vertically to check for excess flowing. It is best to match your test pieces to your pottery style to ensure that the tests are as useful as possible.

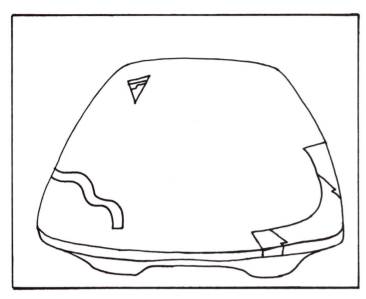

C/6   White Body   Platter   Date

1. Wollastonite Albany green over the whole platter, dipped.
2. Brutus blue in the center, sprayed.
3. G.K. white lightly sprayed at the edge of the platter.

6-70   Notebook entry for a cone 6 white body

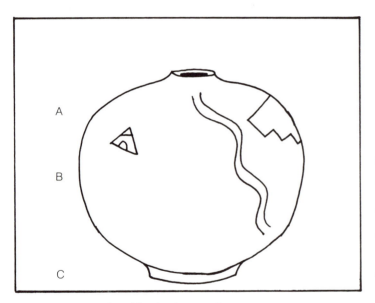

A

B

C

C/6   Stoneware   Vase   Date

1. Wollastonite Albany black glaze inside, poured.
2. Iron solution sprayed over the whole pot, especially heavy from A to B.
3. G.K. white glaze sprayed over the vase, especially heavy at the lip and point A.
4. Wollastonite Albany mustard sprayed in a band below point B.

6-71   Notebook entry for a cone 6 stoneware vase

222

Appendix

Due to economic and geographic factors, many potters who use this book will not have access to some of the specific materials called for in my clay body and glaze formulas. This section has been created to help the potter find acceptable substitutes.

There are great differences in the way that clays and glaze materials are distributed and sold. While most glazes are widely available, clays have a much more limited pattern of commercial distribution. Clay is a heavy material, economical to produce but uneconomical to ship. Furthermore, clays are found all over the world and there are locally-available versions of most common types. This is especially true of stoneware clays (also known as plastic fire clays), high iron clays and coarse particled clays.

The situation varies in each locale and so must be discussed in terms of regions. For each area, I will suggest locally available materials that could serve as equivalents or substitutes for those called for in my formulas.

Obviously, if substitutes are employed, your results may not be quite like mine. I have tried to match the alternative materials to the originals as closely as possible, and I believe that, generally, your versions of my formulas will be useful and beautiful. However, I urge you to perform tests on these adapted formulas before committing yourself to their extensive use.

The following materials may be unavailable in your region:

Clays:
    Cedar Heights Redart clay
    P.B.X. fire clay
    Cedar Heights Goldart stoneware clay

Pine Lake fire clay
OM 4 ball clay, Tennessee ball clay, XX Sagger ball clay
A.P. Green fire clay
Six Tile kaolin
Velvacast kaolin

Glaze clays:
Albany slip clay
Barnard slip clay

Melters:
Gerstley borate
Hommel frit 90, Ferro frit 3124

I will suggest appropriate alternatives for these materials for potters in the Western United States, Canada, and Great Britain. These are the regions of the world for which this book is primarily intended. For those potters who live in other places, the equivalency chart contains information which may be used as a general guide so that you may choose, with the aid of your materials supplier, appropriate substitutes. This chart will also enable potters to integrate materials that I have not mentioned for one reason or another.

Readers outside the United States should note that I often refer to a type of clay known as "stoneware." While the use of this term is quite common throughout the world when applied to clay bodies, it is rarely used to refer to a raw clay except in the United States. When I refer to a stoneware *clay*, I refer to a raw clay which matures at about cone 8 or 9 (1263°–1280°C), is buff- or tan-colored in the oxidation fire, and, because of its high fine particle content, is quite plastic. As the name would imply, this sort of clay is well suited for use in stoneware bodies but it is not limited to that function, for it also works very well in fineclay and low fire bodies. Outside of the United States, clays that fall into this category are often termed "plastic fireclays."

GENERAL EQUIVALENCIES

	Suggested Material	Significant Ingredients	Percentage	What to Look for in an Equivalent
Clays	Cedar Heights Redart	silica alumina iron	64.2 16.4 7.0	high iron, fine particled, low temperature maturation, red firing
	P.B.X. fire clay	silica alumina iron	66.0 24.0 1.5	high iron, coarse particled, fairly high maturation, orange or tan firing
	Cedar Heights Goldart stoneware	silica alumina iron	57.3 28.5 1.2	medium low iron, mostly fine particled, high maturation, tan or buff firing

224

	Pine Lake fire clay	silica	66.0	fairly low iron, coarse particled, high maturation, oyster, buff or tan firing
		alumina	22.0	
		iron	1.2	
Ball clays	Kentucky OM 4 Tennessee XX Sagger	silica	53.8	low iron, very plastic, high shrinkage, high maturation, buff, tan or ivory firing
		alumina	30.0	
		iron	0.9	
	A. P. Green fire clay	silica	50.0	low iron, coarse particled, high maturation, tan, ivory or buff firing
		alumina	30.0	
		iron	1.0	
	Six Tile kaolin	silica	47.0	very low iron, non-plastic, fine particled, very high maturation, white firing
		alumina	37.0	
		iron	0.5	
	Velvacast kaolin	silica	45.4	coarse particled, very high maturation, non-plastic, kaolin
		alumina	38.9	
		iron	0.3	
Glaze clays	Albany slip clay	silica	57.6	common red clay or terra cotta, low firing, high impurity, dark firing
		alumina	14.6	
		iron	5.2	
		calcium	5.7	
		sodium/ potassium	4.0	
	Barnard slip clay	silica	52.4	common red clay or terra cotta, low firing, high impurity, dark firing
		alumina	10.6	
		iron	20.3	
		potassium	3.7	
		manganese	3.2	
Melters	Gerstley borate	boron	28.0	boron calcium frit, low in silica and alumina
		calcium	20.0	
		sodium/ potassium	5.0	
	Frit 3124 or 90	silica	54.8	boron calcium frit, fairly high silica and sodium/ potassium content
		alumina	9.7	
		boron	13.9	
		calcium	13.9	
		potassium	6.3	

Great Britain

CLAYS

As you will note in the materials substitution chart for Great Britain, there are clays available in the U.K. which will substitute very nicely for the clays in my formulas.

I feel that I need to discuss only Cedar Heights Redart, for there is no exact substitute for this low firing red clay in Great Britain. The following blend has been suggested as a suitable alternative:

Etruria Red Clay	85%
Potash Feldspar	15%

GLAZE CLAYS

Albany slip clay. There is no exact equivalent for this high impurity clay in the U.K. However, two high impurity materials are widely available which have some similarity to Albany: Fremington clay and Etruria Red Clay. Fremington may be used as a one-for-one substitute for Albany slip clay; Etruria requires borax and iron additions (see chart).

Barnard slip clay. Here again there is no exact equivalent, but basalt (a high impurity feldspar) is very similar, especially if used with an iron addition.

MELTERS

Frit 3124 (Ferro U.S.A.) and 90 (Hommel). Podmore's Frit 2245 appears to be quite similar and should substitute very closely.

Gerstley borate. The problem here is much more complex and the origin of the problem is very interesting. Both gerstley borate and certain British frits are substitutes for the powerful but unpredictable material colemanite. Since they are both substitutes for the same material, it stands to reason that they would be very similar and could serve as reliable substitutes for each other. Unfortunately, however, this is not always true. While both the U.S. and the U.K. materials contain calcium and boron, they differ significantly in other ways. Gerstley borate contains some sodium, while the boro-calcium frits used in the U.K. contain some alumina and silica. In many formulas, these differences will have little impact, and the boro-calcium frits will substitute in a completely satisfactory manner for gerstley borate. If, however, the substitution is unsuccessful, the glaze will be immature. In this case, I recommend trying the following:

1. Blend, in equal parts, frits 2244 (Podmore) or 2268 (Potclays) with frit 2245 (Podmore). Frit 2245 has a significant sodium/potassium content. In certain formulas, this blend may be a better substitute for gerstley borate than the boro-calcium frit used alone.

2. Blend frits 2244 (Podmore) or 2268 (Potclays) with 20 percent of a high

alkaline frit such as Podmore's 2275, or with a high alkaline feldspar such as nepheline syenite.

I obtained samples of Podmore's frits 2244 and 2245, and tested them in a number of cone 6 formulas with which I was quite familiar. I used two of the procedures suggested above. First, I simply substituted 2244 for gerstley borate; second, I substituted an equal amount of 2244 and 2245 for gerstley borate.

The results, I think, were quite good (partly owing to my preference for complex multi-ingredient glaze formulas in which no one material is likely to be absolutely crucial). Out of seven formulas tested, only one produced unusable results. In the others, one or both substitute formulations proved to be quite satisfactory. The results are as follows:

Glaze	Results with 2244	Results with 2244/2245
Troy II	A good glaze, though somewhat shinier than the original	A very good glaze. It is satin surfaced, smooth and enamel-like
Zakin Base	Only fair. Somewhat rough and unstable	A very good glaze with a smooth, rich satin surface and good color
Coburg Base	Quite a good glaze with a rich, smooth, satin surface	A good glaze with a durable satin mat surface
Cardington Base	Slightly immature	Also slightly immature
Satin Mat I	An excellent glaze with a rich satin mat surface	An excellent glaze but quite unlike the original; shiny, transparent, and very durable
Gower Base	Slightly immature	A good glaze with a smooth, enamel-like surface
Chenies Base	Rough where thin but fairly useful otherwise	A very good glaze with a rich mat surface

MATERIALS SUBSTITUTION, GREAT BRITAIN

	Original Material	Suggested Equivalent	Percentage	Source
Clays	Cedar Heights Redart	Etruria Red Clay Potash feldspar	85 15	Potclays, Podmore
	P.B.X. fire clay	Roche clay	100	Potclays
	Cedar Heights Goldart stoneware	N 6 clay	100	Potclays
	Pine Lake fire clay	N 5 clay	100	Potclays
Ball clays	Kentucky Tennessee XX Sagger	Hymod smd or Hvar	100	Potclays, Podmore
	A. P. Green	N 5 clay	100	Potclays
	Six Tile kaolin	Grolleg, Gunheath, Trevisco	100	English china clay
	Velvacast kaolin	Eobby clay	100	Potclays
Glaze clays	Albany slip clay	Etruria Red Clay borax iron	50 45 5	Podmore, Potclays, etc.
		Fremington clay	100	
	Barnard slip clay	basalt iron	88 12	Podmore, Potclays, etc.
Melters	Gerstley borate	Frit 2244 or Frit 2268 with 2245	see text	Podmore, Potclays
	Hommel Frit 90, Ferro Frit 3124	Frit 2245	100	Podmore

The Western United States

There are not many potters who are enthusiastic about the expensive process of shipping clay over the Rocky Mountains. As a result, potters on the West Coast tend to use Western clays if they can. Ball clays and kaolins are shipped in from the east, but locally mined clays are used otherwise.

The Muddox Company in Sacramento, California, mines and processes a complete line of iron-bearing clays. Their list includes a stoneware clay and two fire clays, one fairly low in iron, the other high. While their fire clays are of the medium-silica-type rather than the high-silica-type represented by Pine Lake, a mixture of Muddox #1 (75 percent) and ground silica or flint (25 percent) should work very well as a substitute. This same strategy will work if you wish to substitute Lincoln fire clay or Green Stripe fire clay, both popular in the West, for Pine Lake.

Glaze materials present no problems. A number of supply houses stock a complete line of glaze materials including all of those that I call for.

MATERIALS SUBSTITUTION, WESTERN UNITED STATES

Original Material	Suggested Equivalent	Percentage	Source
Cedar Heights Redart	Newman clay	75	Muddox Clay Co.
	Potash feldspar	25	
	E M 207 clay	100	WCS Co.
Cedar Heights Goldart stoneware clay	Buena Vista	100	Muddox Clay Co.
A. P. Green fire clay	#1 clay	100	Muddox Clay Co.
Pine Lake fire clay	#1 clay	75	Muddox Clay Co.
	flint	25	
P.B.X. fire clay	Newman clay	100	Muddox Clay Co.

Canada

EASTERN CANADA

In this region, ball clays and kaolins are imported from the United States and England. A great many other clays are imported from the U.S. as well. Therefore, the clays I call for are generally available. There are, however, Canadian equivalents for many of these clays. They are listed in the chart next to their U.S. counterparts.

Original Material	Suggested Equivalent	Source
Cedar Heights Redart	Minac Red Clay	The Pottery Supply House
P.B.X. fire clay	Musquodoboit	The Pottery Supply House
Cedar Heights Goldart	Shubenacadie	The Pottery Supply House
Pine Lake fire clay	Shubenacadie coarse grind	The Pottery Supply House

The standard list of North American glaze materials is widely available in Canada.

WESTERN CANADA

The situation in Western Canada is similar to that of the Western U.S. Potters use local clays if they can. The standard glaze materials are readily available.

Plainsman Clays mine and sell a line of raw clays, as well as the prepared clay bodies for which they are well known. These raw clays can be used as substitutes for the ones I use in my formulas. Potters in Western Canada might consider contacting Plainsman Clays for suggested substitutes for individual materials.

I wish to acknowledge the help the following materials supply houses:

UNITED STATES:

The Archie Bray Foundation
Country Club Avenue
Helena, Montana 59601
(406) 442-2521

H.C. Muddox Clay Company
5875 Bradshaw Road
Sacramento, California 95826
(916) 362-1171

Seattle Pottery Supplies
400 E. Pine Street
Seattle, Washington 98122
(206) 324-4343

WCS Pottery Equipment and Supplies
14400 Lomitas Avenue Dept. B017
City Of Industry, California 91746
(213) 330-0631

CANADA:

The Pottery Supply House Limited
P.O. Box 192
Oakville, Ontario L6J 5AZ
(416) 827-1129

The Green Barn Potters Supply
P.O. Box 1235 Station A
Surrey, British Columbia
(604) 888-3411

Plainsman Clays Limited
Box 1266
Medicine Hat, Alberta T1A 7M9
(403) 527-8535

UNITED KINGDOM:

Podmore Ceramics Limited
105 Minet Road
London SW9 7UH
01-737-3636

and

Podmore & Sons Limited
Shelton, Stoke-on-Trent
Staffordshire, England
0782-24571

Potclays Limited
Brickkiln Lane, Etruria
Stoke-on-Trent, England
0782-29816

Ferro Great Britain
Ownsdale Road, Wombourne
Wolverhampton, England WV5 8DA
902-89-4144

Glossary

Alumina: One of the basic building blocks of clays and glazes. The alumina-containing glaze materials are clays and feldspars. Alumina promotes plasticity and strength in clay bodies, and durability and viscosity in glazes. Glazes with a high alumina content tend to be mat, opaque, non-running and very durable.

A. P. Green fire clay: The trade name of a coarse, large-particled fire clay which contributes strength and workability. It is quite plastic and fairly light in color, containing 1 percent iron and 1.5 percent titanium.

Bisque firing: A preliminary firing of unglazed ware. While bisque firing temperatures may vary widely, it is most common to bisque fire to cones 08–04. When fired in this way, the ware will absorb the water in which the glazes are suspended without being weakened.

Calcine: To purify a substance using heat. The impurities, generally water or carbon, are driven off as gases. Calcined materials are used to make formulas purer, more stable or more useful. For example, in high clay glazes the plasticity of the clay may cause difficulties during firing; calcining is used to diminish the plasticity.

Cedar Heights Goldart: The trade name of a stoneware clay known for its workability and strength. Clay bodies which contain Goldart tend to be buff, tan or ochre in color due to the iron (1.23 percent) and titanium (1.98 percent) in the formula. Goldart also contains a significant sulfur impurity, requiring a well-ventilated kiln area (a reasonable precaution in any case).

Cedar Heights Redart: The trade name of a high iron clay. Due to its impurities, this clay is only moderately workable and durable, but the impurities, including 7 percent iron, promote rich, hearty clay body colors. This clay is often used as an ingredient to darken clay bodies and encourage maturity.

Clay body: A compound of clay and non-clay materials chosen for their individual characteristics that, when combined, meet the specific requirements of the ceramist.

Colorant: A mineral or compound of minerals used to color ceramic materials. The most common colorants are: iron oxide, cobalt oxide or carbonate, copper carbonate, rutile (a compound of titanium and iron), and manganese dioxide.

Crawling: A glaze defect in which the glaze forms in separate droplets during firing rather than in a smooth durable surface. When this phenomenon occurs on a dust- or dirt-free bisque fired piece, it generally indicates that the glaze formula is too viscous, due to an overly high alumina content. In this case, the clay content of the glaze must be lowered.

Deflocculant: An alkaline material which encourages clay particles to repel each other.

Deflocculated: Lowered or entirely negated clay plasticity. Clay bodies which have been somewhat deflocculated (generally by alkaline melters in the formula) lose much of their plasticity. Clay which has been highly deflocculated becomes a completely non-plastic material, used in slip-casting to make high clay content bodies which are liquid.

Engobe: Originally, this term was related to the concept of an envelope—that is, an overall coating of slip. Slips used as engobes were almost always porcelain slips intended to disguise modest clay bodies so that they might be confused with porcelains. The term has come to mean a porcelain or semi-porcelain slip applied in any fashion. Engobes have a clay content of 25 to 50 percent and a non-clay content of 50 to 75 percent.

E. P. K. Kaolin: A trade name of a Florida (U.S.A.) kaolin. It is very pure, containing 0.42 percent iron and 0.34 percent titanium. E. P. K. is quite low in plasticity, perhaps better used as a glaze clay than as a body clay, especially where the body must be plastic and workable. E. P. K. is quite refractory, a trait common to all kaolins.

Filler: A neutral material. Clay body fillers are non-plastic additions generally used to increase strength and lower shrinkage. Their particle size varies from very coarse to very fine. Fillers for slips, engobes and glazes are finely ground, non-melting, non-clay materials, employed to strengthen and stabilize the formula.

Fineclay: A clay body whose clay content varies from 65 to 85 percent and whose non-clay content varies from 35 to 15 percent. These bodies have been formulated to have much of the strength and workability of stoneware and much of the richness and refinement of porcelain. Fineclays vary greatly in color, ranging from white to dark brown.

Flocculant: An acidic material which encourages the aggregation of clay particles.

Flocculate: To cause clay aggregation by the addition of acidic materials.

Flocculated: A state in which clay particles tend to aggregate or clump together;

the clay mass acts as a coherent, workable material that can be shaped and formed.

Flux: An oxide that causes melting, including the oxides of barium, calcium, boron, sodium, potassium, and silicon.

Frit: Manufactured compounds containing silica, alumina and melters. While more expensive than many materials which find use in ceramics, they are highly valued and used widely for their stabilizing and strong melting powers.

Frit 90 (Hommel), Frit 3124 (Ferro), Frit P-311 (Pemco): These three frits are almost identical in makeup and character. Their silica content is high and their alumina content fairly low. Calcium and boron are the main melting ingredients. It is probable that these are the most commonly used frits for mid- and high-fire ceramic use in the United States. Any good ceramic supply house will stock at least one.

Glaze: A glassy coating especially formulated to fit over a clay form. Glazes contain silica, alumina and melter.

Grit: A term sometimes used for large-particled fillers.

Gritware: Clay bodies with an unusually high grog or grit content (40–50 percent).

Grog: A coarse-particled filler for clay bodies. The presence of grog ensures that the clay body will contain a wide variety of particle sizes. Grog also impedes warping and encourages durability.

Kaolin: Clay distinguished by its great purity and whiteness. Kaolins tend to be less easily worked than other clays but this difficulty is compensated for by their beauty and refined character.

Majolica: A brilliantly colored glaze painting technique employing majolica glazes. This technique was extensively used in European ceramics in the 15th and 16th centuries.

Majolica glaze: A low-fire glaze type, the main ingredients of which are lead oxide (a strong melter) and tin oxide (an opacifier). Often strongly colored.

Melter: A compound that causes melting, facilitating glaze formation. Melters include silicates, feldspars, and fluxes.

Opacifier: A material which blocks the passage of light through the glaze, thereby rendering the glaze opaque. This action usually takes the form of small bubbles trapped under the surface of the glaze or of crystals which change the structure of the glaze.

Opax: The trade name of a comparatively pure and powerful zirconium opacifier. Generally, additions of 10 to 12 percent are sufficient to ensure complete opacity.

Oxidation: The combination of a material with oxygen.

Oxidation firing: Allowing ready access of oxygen to the firing chamber at all times. Generally, electric kilns are constructed in such a way as to fire in oxidation.

P.B.X. Fire Clay (also known as *Valentine Fire Clay*): The trade name of a coarse-particled high iron fire clay, generally used in amounts of 12–14 percent in clay bodies. It promotes workability and rich color.

Pine Lake Fire Clay: The trade name of a coarse-particled fire clay. It contributes strength and workability. Its color is fairly light, for it contains little more

234

than 1 percent iron and 1½ percent titanium. Because Pine Lake is a high silica material, clay bodies containing it may need a less than normal amount of ground silica (flint).

Plasticizer: An ingredient added to a formula to improve workability. Two types are available: super fine-particled clay plasticizers and organic plasticizers. Super fine-particled clays (such as bentonite) increase the variety of particle sizes in the clay body. Organic plasticizers (such as yogurt or beer) act as lubricants and encourage the easy movement of particles.

Porcelain: A pure white clay body that is translucent where thin, named after the translucent white Venus sea shell (*porcellus* in Latin). Most porcelains are high-fired (cone 9 and above) and have a non-clay content which is equal or nearly equal to the clay content. These clay bodies contain only white or colorless materials. Because of their low clay content and the purity of their ingredients, porcelains are not very workable.

Powdered silica (flint): A white, finely ground crystalline powder. An important source of silica in the glaze.

Reduction firing: Firing with a minimum amount of oxygen. In reduction firing, the potter interrupts the flow of adequate oxygen to the firing chamber of the kiln at certain crucial periods during the firing. This is most naturally accomplished in the fuel-burning kiln. Reduction firing strongly influences the character of clay bodies and glazes.

Refractory: Resistant to heat.

Rutile: A colorant compound of iron and titanium.

Salt firing: A specialized type of firing in fuel-burning kilns especially con- structed for the purpose. Salt (sodium chloride) is introduced into the kiln chamber through openings in its walls toward the end of the firing. The salt reacts to the heat of the firing and literally explodes. A coating of sodium covers all the ware in the kiln. Sodium is a powerful melter; it combines with the silica and alumina in the clay body to produce a glaze on the surface of the ware. This glaze is often marked with a rich, light and dark texture called "orange peel" that seems to be a product of the violence of the reaction.

Shivering: Glaze patches forced away from the ware, leaving sections of un- glazed body visible; most easily observed at the corners and edges of the piece. Shivering occurs when the glaze shrinks less than the body upon which it rests. It can be eliminated by increasing the shrinkage of the glaze or by decreasing the shrinkage of the clay body.

Silica: A crystalline material that, along with alumina, is one of the building blocks of all clays and glazes. The sources of silica are powdered silica, feldspars, clays and silicates (talc and wollastonite). Silica promotes plasticity and durability in clay bodies, and glaze flow, durability and a glassy melt in glaze formulas.

Six Tile kaolin: The trade name of a Georgia (U.S.A.) kaolin. This very finely ground clay is extremely workable. When fired in oxidation, its color is slightly creamy due to its high titanium content (1.42 percent). Like all kaolins, Six Tile is fairly refractory.

Slip: A mixture of clay and water used to hold clay pieces together. Also, a mixture of clay (or clays) and water, with perhaps some non-clay materials, that is applied to the surface of the clay piece for decorative effect. Since slips are high in clay, they may be applied before the first firing, while the piece is still moist. In this way the clay piece and the slip will dry at the same time and will bond and fire well together.

Soft paste porcelain: Traditionally, porcelain is fired to very high temperatures of 1300°C or more (cones 9–12). Porcelain fired to lower temperatures must contain very strong melters (due to the refractory character of the clay content of porcelain); these strong melters unfortunately deprive porcelain of the dense and durable qualities for which it is so admired. These softer, less dense, highly fluxed clay bodies are termed soft paste porcelain to distinguish them from the real thing.

Stains: Calcined compounds of various colorants formulated to produce rich saturated color. Stains may be used to color clay bodies, slips, engobes and glazes, under, in or on surfaces. Since stains may be used in so many ways, in association with so many different materials, at so many different firing temperatures, it is important to try a new stain or stain technique on test pieces so that any problems may be solved before good pieces are spoiled.

Stoneware clay: A term used in the United States to designate a raw clay that matures at cones 8–9, is buff or tan color in oxidation, and is plastic and workable.

Stoneware clay body: A body that contains a high percentage of clay and a low percentage of non-clay materials (some stoneware bodies contain no non-clay materials whatsoever). The clays used generally contain some iron and titanium impurities (3–4 percent), and so tend to be earthy and hearty in character. In color, stoneware bodies are buff, tan, orange or brown. They are very workable and durable, maturing at cones 6–11.

Talc body: A clay body which contains a significant amount of talc (usually 25 to 50 percent). Talc is a strong melter and is especially useful in low and mid fire clay bodies. Talc clay bodies tend to be fairly workable.

Terra cotta: The most common form of clay, found in most parts of the world. Terra cotta is a high impurity clay because it is a product of erosion. It is generally gray or ochre in color before firing and red in color after firing (derived from iron oxide). Terra cottas mature at a low temperature; they are usually fired in oxidation to take advantage of their rich earth-red fired color.

Velvacast: The trade name of a kaolin from Georgia (U.S.A.). It is unusual because it is coarsely ground. Velvacast promotes workability in porcelains in a way that is similar to the action of a fireclay in non-porcelain bodies.

White body: A clay body containing only white and colorless clay and non-clay materials. Porcelain bodies are a type of white body; they are high fire and translucent, but other white bodies may be opaque or intended for the lower fire.

White stoneware: An opaque white clay body. These bodies, like porcelain, must contain only white or colorless materials such as kaolins, ball clays, and non-iron bearing melters. Unlike porcelain, they may have a fairly high clay to non-clay ratio, and tend to be much more workable than porcelain. This term is somewhat narrow and unhelpful. I prefer the new term "white fineclay," because these clay bodies are not stoneware and do not look or feel like stoneware.

Whiting (calcium carbonate): A melter of fairly low power. It is used in slips, engobes and glazes, and occasionally in clay bodies. In both clays and glazes it promotes durability; in glazes it also may promote rich glaze surfaces.

Zirconium opacifiers: A group of similar compounds, all containing the element zirconium, which interferes with the passage of light in glazes. Not all zirconium opacifiers are of equal purity or opacifying power. However, all tend to produce similar results, and substitutions between various zirconium opacifiers are often successful.

Zircopax: The trade name of an economical zirconium opacifier which contains a significant percentage of silica. This impurity interferes with its opacifying action in some formulas.

Index

8272